MASSEE'S
WINE-FOOD
INDEX

by
WILLIAM E. MASSEE
Drawings by Dorothy Ivens

Bramhall House · New York

This edition published by
Bramhall House, a division of
Clarkson N. Potter, Inc., by arrangement
with the author
c d e f g h

MASSEE'S
WINE-FOOD
INDEX

Books by William E. Massee

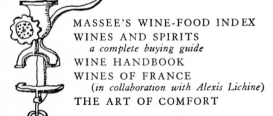

MASSEE'S WINE-FOOD INDEX
WINES AND SPIRITS
 a complete buying guide
WINE HANDBOOK
WINES OF FRANCE
 (*in collaboration with Alexis Lichine*)
THE ART OF COMFORT

to
Felix

CONTENTS

outstanding
RESTAURANTS
whose menus have been used
in the preparation of this book

AUSTRIA
VIENNA
Zu den 3 Husaren
SALZBURG
Goldener Hirsch

BELGIUM
BRUSSELS
La Couronne

DENMARK
COPENHAGEN
Au Coq d'Or
Krog's
7 Nations

ENGLAND
LONDON
Bentley's
Isola Bella
L'Ecu de France
Mirabelle
Wheeler's
BRIGHTON
Mascotte

FRANCE
PARIS
Avignon
Berkeley Hotel
Lapérouse
Lasserre
La Tour d'Argent
Le Grand Vefour
Maxim's
Taillevent
THESSEY
Le Chapon Fin
AVIGNON
Lucullus
VILLENEUVE DE
    MARSAN
    (south of Bordeaux)
Darroze
STRASBOURG
Valentine Sorg
SAULIEU
Hôtel de la Côte d'Or

GERMANY
BERLIN
Ritz
ASSMANSHAUSEN
Hotel Krone

HOLLAND
THE HAGUE
Restaurant Saur
Tampat Senang
AMSTERDAM
Victoria Hotel

IRELAND
DUBLIN
Jammet
The Russell
The Shelbourne

ITALY
ROME
Alfredo
Doney
Hostaria dell' Orso
Passetto
MILAN
Savini
FLORENCE
Buca Lapi
Sabatini
BOLOGNA
al Pappagallo

PORTUGAL
LISBON
Aviz Hotel
Óh Lacerda

SPAIN
MADRID
Botín
Ritz Hotel

UNITED STATES
 • *CALIFORNIA*
LOS ANGELES
General Lee's
Mandarin Room
    of Man Jen Low
Oyster House
SAN FRANCISCO
Amelio's
Ernie's
Kan's
The Blue Fox
Trader Vic's
 • *DISTRICT OF
    COLUMBIA*
WASHINGTON
Place Vendome
Rive Gauche
 • *FLORIDA*
MIAMI BEACH
Gaucho Steak House,
    Americana Hotel
DANIA
Le Cordon Bleu
BAL HARBOUR
Americana
PALM BEACH
Petite Marmite
 • *HAWAII*
HONOLULU
Canlis' Charcoal Broiler
 • *ILLINOIS*
CHICAGO
Blackhawk
Cafe de Paris
Pump Room
The Drake
 • *KENTUCKY*
LEXINGTON
Campbell House
LOUISVILLE
The Old House
 • *LOUISIANA*
NEW ORLEANS
Antoine's
Galatoire's

Owen Brennan's
The Pontchartrain
 • *MARYLAND*
BALTIMORE
Miller Brothers
 • *MASSACHUSETTS*
BOSTON
Loch-Ober Cafe
 • *MICHIGAN*
DETROIT
London Chop House
MARSHALL
Schuler's
 • *MISSOURI*
LADUE
Busch's Grove
 • *NEBRASKA*
OMAHA
Orleans Room,
 Blackstone Hotel
 •*NEVADA*
RENO
Eugene's
 • *NEW JERSEY*
Ho-ho-kus Inn
 • *NEW YORK*
Baroque
Chateaubriand
Forum of the
 Twelve Caesars
La Côte Basque
L'Aiglon
Le Crémaillère
 à la Campagne
Le Pavillon
Quo Vadis
San Marino
The Four Seasons
Twenty-one
Voisin
BROOKLYN
Gage & Tollner's

BETHPAGE, LONG
 ISLAND
Beau Sejour
 • *OHIO*
CINCINNATI
Gourmet Restaurant
Pigall's
Terrace Hilton
SHAKER HEIGHTS
Gruber's
 • *OREGON*
PORTLAND
The Benson
 • *PENNSYLVANIA*
PHILADELPHIA
The Barclay
PITTSBURGH
Park Schenley
 • *TEXAS*
DALLAS
Mario's
SAN ANTONIO
La Louisiane
 • *WASHINGTON*
SEATTLE
Canlis' Charcoal Broiler

MASSEE'S
WINE-FOOD
INDEX

WINES

Red *wines* taste best with meat, fowl and cheese. Full wines like Burgundies and Rhônes go best with hearty dishes like roasts and stews, game, and those with rich sauces. Lighter reds or old wines like Bordeaux and Côte d'Or Burgundies bring out the flavors of grilled foods and those with subtle savors or delicate sauces. Fruity young reds like Beaujolais or Chinon go best with simple dishes or those with light but spicy flavors, like a broiled steak or a chicken casserole.

White wines taste best with fish and sea food, all kinds of cold cuts and delicatessen. Burgundy whites, dry and full, taste best with freshwater fish, meat and fowl served with white sauces, and lightly smoked or spiced foods. Flowery whites like Graves, Loire, or Rhine wines taste best with spicily sauced fish and fowl dishes, with fat or starchy dishes, such as *pastas* or fish stews.

Rosé wines go with anything, as do Champagnes or *Sparkling wines*, but are best with white wine dishes.

Fortified wines taste best before and after meals, although dry Sherries are good with rich sea food and ham dishes, or

1

spicy Oriental foods. Ports and Madeiras and Oloroso Sherries taste best with melons and other flavorsome fruits, with cakes and puddings, nuts and cheeses, after a meal.

Index
of Wines

Abboccato [ahb-bok-*kah*-to]
Italian term for sweetish as applied to wine, opposed to *secco*, dry.

Acidity
Fruit acids, collectively called the *fixed acidity* of a wine, impart a fresh and zesty taste. Light wines from mild climates (lower Italy, California) tend to lack this acidity and to taste bland or flat, while light northern wines (Switzerland, New York) tend to have too much, tasting sharp or tart. When a wine oxidizes, acetic acid forms; called the *volatile acidity* of a wine, it turns a wine sour, so this oxidation is curtailed in good wine-making.

Ahr
River that joins the Rhine near Bonn, whose valley vineyards, like those in Walporzheim, produce small, light reds.

Albana [ahl-*bah*-nah]
Good, fruity white from Emilia, fine with *pasta*, fish and sea food, ham and pork dishes. Dry Albana is best.

Albano [ahl-*bah*-no]
Good dry white from Rome's Alban hills, to go with *pasta*, ham and sausages, pork and veal dishes, fish and sea food.

Alcohol

Alcohols, which impart roundness, fullness, and liveliness of taste to a wine, are formed along with carbon dioxide during fermentation, as a result of the action of yeasts on the sugars in the juice of freshly squeezed grapes. The natural fruit acids in the wine continue to work on its alcohols to break down parts of them into esters, which have more subtle flowery smells and tastes than the alcohols. Naturally fermented wines usually vary from 9 to 14 per cent alcohol, and are called *light wines* or *table wines*. Some wines have brandy added to them to hold them to desired tastes; these, called *fortified wines*, include Sherry, Port, and Madeira, and range generally from 14 to 21 per cent alcohol. *Aromatic wines* are those which have herbs and spices added (Vermouth, Maiwein). *Sparkling wines* like Champagne are produced when the carbon dioxide formed during fermentation is retained in the wine; these are usually around 12 per cent alcohol.

Aleatico [ah-leh-*ah*-tee-ko]
Heavy, sweetish red from Tuscany, good on Elba.

Alella [ah-*leh*-lyah]
Flowery, sweetish white from near Barcelona.

Alicante-Bouschet [ah-lee-*kahn*-teh-boo-*sheh*]
Poor red wine grape producing miserable muck.

Aloxe-Corton [ah-loss-kor-tawn]
Burgundy town producing full reds and whites, Corton and Corton Charlemagne being outstanding. Serve reds with roasts and grillades of meat, fowl, game. Serve whites with fish and sea food, veal, ham, pork dishes.

Alsace [ahl-zass]
French region along the Rhine producing flowery whites from Gewürz-Traminer, Traminer, Riesling, and Sylvaner grapes, and so called on labels; blends from these are called Edelzwicker.

Best townships are in Bas-Rhin, between Colmar and Sélestat:

Ammerschwihr	Kientzheim	Ribeauvillé
Bergheim	Mittelwihr	Riquewihr
Kaysersberg		

Serve with fish like trout, sausages and delicatessen, ham, pork, and cheese dishes.

Amoroso [ah-mo-*ro*-so]
Name used in England, primarily, for lightly sweetened Spanish Oloroso Sherries. Good with biscuits, cakes, melons.

Angelica [an-*jel*-ee-kah]
A cheap, syrupy mixture of grape juice and alcohol made in California.

Anjou [ahn-zhoo]
Anjou lends its name to a multitude of wines, fruity, light whites made from the Chenin Blanc grape and *rosés* with an orange tint made from the Cabernet in vineyards around the city of Angers, as well as to wines from adjoining districts along the Loire, between the dry-white district of Muscadet, which is near the river's mouth, and the red-wine districts of Chinon and Bourgeuil, toward Tours. Coteaux de Saumur is famous for sweet, full, sparkling whites; Coteaux du Layon is noted for sweet, full whites, especially Quart de Chaume; Coteaux de l'Aubance produces excellent *rosés*; Coteaux de la Loire is noted for flowery whites high in alcohol, particularly from vineyards around Savennières; Coteaux du Loir produces some pleasant *rosés*. There are some 14,000 producers in Anjou, making wines that taste fine in the afternoon, with or without food; they also taste good with lunches and light courses of fish and sea food, ham and cold cuts, creamed dishes and spicy casseroles, aspics and galantines. The whites are perfect with smoked salmon and tongue, the *rosés* with pork, veal, and chicken dishes.

Appellation Contrôlée [ah-pel-lah-syawn kawn-tro-lay]
The only alternate permissible phrase to *Appellation d'Origine* (below) that can be used to identify a wine produced under the

French vineyard control laws. This phrase always appears in conjunction with the place name under whose laws the wine has been produced.

Appellation d'Origine   [ah-pel-lah-syawn dor-ee-zheen]
Name of origin is the phrase by which wines are identified in accordance with the French vineyard control laws, which define the limits of regions, districts, townships, and vineyards, as well as specifying the grapes that can be grown, the ways they must be tended, and how the wines should be made. The phrase is a guarantee of an authentic wine, although not necessarily a guarantee of quality. It is the first thing to look for on a French wine label; if the phrase is not there, the wine has not met any accepted legal standards. Note that the more specific the label, the more restricted are the control laws. A label that reads simply "Burgundy" merely indicates that the wine is from that region, and is entitled only to that appellation. A label that reads "Chambertin Clos de Bèze," however, indicates that the wine is from that specific vineyard in the Burgundy township of Gevrey-Chambertin. Both wines may come under the control laws, but the Chambertin is from a great vineyard, while the mere Burgundy is certain to be nondescript. A wine takes the most specific designation it is entitled to under the control laws, and the above distinction is all-important in buying French wines.

Arbois   [ahr-bwah]
The *rosé* from this township in the mountains of the Jura is considered one of the best of France, perhaps second only to Tavel because of its lightness, and a perfect wine with fish or sea food served with a sauce, with terrines or *pâtés*, with creamed or spicy dishes, with pork or veal preparations.

Artisan   [ahr-tee-zahn]
Name applied to many minor vineyards of the Médoc; the term *Crus Artisans*, Artisan Growths, is used mostly for blends of regional wines. They rank below the so-called *Bourgeois Supérieur* Growths, which are frequently château-bottled.

Assmannshausen [ahs-mahns-*how*-zen]
One of the best German red wines comes from this town down the Rhine from Rüdesheim, made from the Burgundy Pinot Noir, here called Spätburgunder. It is fresh and light, sometimes equal to a lesser Beaune red.

Auslese [*ows*-lay-zuh]
The word means "selection" in German; it is applied to wines made from selected bunches of overripe grapes that have been touched by the mold called *Edelfaule* (*pourriture noble* in France). Wines from these grapes are full, fruity, and somewhat sweet. Wine made from berries selected from these bunches is called *Beerenauslese*; that from particularly dried-up berries is called *Trockenbeerenauslese*; these are exceptionally sweet and rare. These wines taste fruity and full by themselves, but are also for festive times and holiday, or with dessert, although the *Auslesen* are good with simply cooked fish, or sweetish delicacies like smoked salmon, lobster, smoked meats, and other rich dishes.

Ausone [oh-zone]
One of the great red wines of Bordeaux, a First Great Growth of St. Emilion, Château Ausone is noted for fullness and bouquet. A perfect wine for roasts and game.

Austria
Generally light, flowery wines like those of Germany; those from the Vienna suburb of Grinzing, Kloster Neuberg, and Gumpoldskirchen, are best known. Serve with fish, sea food, smoked foods, pork and cold cuts.

Avelsbach [*ah*-vulz-bok]
Very dry, light wines of the Trier district of the Mosel, too acid in ordinary years, exceptional in great years like '59. Best vineyard is Herrenberg. Serve with fish, smoked meats.

Ayl [eyel]
Township on the Saar producing very light wines, good only in best years, top vineyard being Kupp.

Badacsony [*bah*-doch-awn-yee]
District near Lake Balaton producing some of the best Hungarian whites, full and sweet, particularly those from the Keknyelü grape. Serve with light desserts.

Baden [*bah*-den]
Badische wines come from vineyards of the Black Forest slopes of southern Germany, and are light and fresh. The fullest come from Kaiserstuhl, are like Alsatian wines, and are made from the Rülander grape, called the Pinot Gris in France. In Markgräflerland, which is the largest district, bland wines are made from the Gutedel—which is the Chasselas in France and the Fendant in Switzerland, where the grape excels. The Ortenau district, across from Strasbourg, produces some good wines from Riesling grapes, as do the vineyards near Baden Baden producing Mauerwein, which is best from Neuweier. Serve with luncheon foods mild in flavor, such as creamed or cheese or ham dishes.

Banyuls [bahn-yül]
A sweet amber wine from the township of that name near the Spanish border, made from the Grenache and often reaching 18 per cent alcohol, considered one of the best French dessert wines, but not much exported.

Barbaresco [bar-bar-*ehs*-ko]
One of the best townships of the Piedmont, producing one of the lightest of the fruity reds from the Nebbiolo grape, excellent for serving with hearty stews and roasts.

Barbera [bar-*beh*-rah]
A Piedmont grape that produces fairly full red wines in Italy, and excellent young wines in California, for serving with light stews and grillades.

Bardolino [bar-do-*lee*-no]
One of the most pleasing light, fruity red wines of northern Italy, from vineyards on Lake Garda, excellent with fish or chicken served in hearty sauces, with Italian veal and pork dishes.

Barolino [bar-oh-*lee*-no]
This "little Barolo" is less full and fruity than the great Barolo of the Italian Piedmont.

Barolo [bar-o-lo]
The great red wine of the Piedmont, produced from the Nebbiolo grape, full in body, fruity when young, very rich when five or six years old. Serve with roasts, game.

Barsac [bar-sak]
The best known township in the Bordeaux sweet-wine district of Sauternes, the best growths being Château Coutet and Château Climens, which produce great dessert wines.

Beaujolais [bo-zho-lay]
The pet of France, the favorite fruity young wine of all the world, past its prime when more than two years old, and perfect with all hearty dishes. A large district in Southern Burgundy, its leading areas are Juliénas, Saint-Amour, Moulin-à-Vent, Chiroubles, Chénas, Fleurie, Morgon, and Brouilly. Serve with dishes that are not prepared with subtle sauces, particularly with simply cooked roasts, steaks, and chops, chicken and turkey, cheese dishes, and stews.

Beaune [bohn]
The capitol of Burgundy's Golden Slope, its vineyards produce light and fruity reds and whites. The reds reach their peak at three or four; the whites are ready to drink two years after the vintage. Best vineyards are Les Fèves and Les Grèves, although

there are dozens of others. Serve with roasts and grillades, with fowl and terrines.

Beerenauslese [bair-en-*ows*-lay-zuh]
Rare sweet white German wines made in great years from grapes selected from overripe bunches. Serve on occasions, alone, or with desserts. See *Auslese*.

Bernkastel [bairn-kahs-el]
The Bernkastelers are the most famous wines of the Mosel, but they are often equaled by other whites from the nearby townships of Piesport, Graach, Wehlen, and Zeltingen. They reach their peak about two years after the vintage, are fruity and well-balanced. Best known vineyards are Doktor, Lay, Rosenberg. Excellent with fish, smoked meats, cold cuts.

Beychevelle [baysh-vel]
A famous Bordeaux red wine from the town of St. Julien in the Médoc, rated as a Fourth Growth a century ago, but considered on a par with Second Growths today. Needs four years or more to mature. Excellent with roasts, grillades, fowl.

Blagny [blahn-yee]
A village in the township of Meursault producing excellent light reds, and whites that are officially sold as Meursault. Reds good with beef, veal, and fowl; whites excellent with fish, ham and pork, delicatessen.

Blanc de blancs [blahn duh blahn]
White of whites, Champagne made solely from the Pinot Chardonnay in the Côte de Blancs section of the Champagne region, the best coming from the towns of Mesnil, Cramant, and Avize. Generally the driest and most austere of the Champagnes, they taste best by themselves or with equally rare caviar or *foie gras*. See *Champagne*.

Blanquette de Limoux [blahn-ket duh lih-moo]
Sweet and pleasant white sparkling wine from a town near Carcassonne.

Bocksbeutel [*box*-boy-tuhl]
The "goat's bottle," so called because of its shape, is the round, pouchy green flask used originally for the flowery white wines of Franconia (Frankenwein or Steinwein) and now for other German wines like Mauerwein, and for Chilean and California whites.

Bodenheim [*bo*-den-hime]
Minor town of the Rheinhessen that produces good wines from the Sylvaner grape to serve with fish, delicatessen, pork, or veal.

Body
Basic wine term. Wines lacking in body taste watery or thin. Wines light in body may not taste watery but taste best when drunk several swallows at a time rather than sipped; the French call such wines *facile à boire,* and these easy-to-drink wines, which include most of the dry or flowery white wines, nearly all pink wines, and reds like Beaujolais, are best suited for everyday drinking. Full-bodied wines, like the fine reds of Bordeaux, Burgundy, and the Rhône, have a rounded-out, winy taste, with little or no wateriness and taste their best when drunk a swallow at a time, or sipped.

Bommes [bom]
Township of the Bordeaux sweet-white-wine district of Sauternes, whose First Growths are the châteaux of Haut-Peyraguey and Lafaurie Peyraguey, Rabaud and Rayne-Vigneau, producing distinguished dessert wines.

Bordeaux [bor-do]
The French wine region that produces more great wines than any other on earth, particularly the dry reds from the districts of the Médoc, St. Emilion, Pomerol, and Graves, the sweet white wines of Sauternes, and the flowery whites of Graves. The best wines are château-bottled; that is, put in bottle at the vineyard by the grower. Those of the Médoc and Sauternes were classified into *crus* or growths by number over a century ago. There are sixty such classed growths in the Médoc; other

Médoc vineyards were later rated as *Crus Exceptionnels* and *Crus Bourgeois Supérieurs,* these Exceptional and Superior Bourgeois Growths generally producing excellent wines. Nine outstanding red-wine vineyards are recognized as the best vineyards today, and are listed in italics. Médoc vineyards are listed here by township, their old ratings following their name, indicated by number or the letter E for Exceptional Growths;

HAUT MÉDOC

MARGAUX & ITS NEIGHBORS

Château
Margaux I
Boyd-Cantenac III
Brane-Cantenac II
Cantemerle V
Cantenac-Brown III
Durfort-Vivens II
Ferrière III
Giscours III
Grand La Lagune III
d'Issan III
Kirwan III

Château
Lascombes II
Malescot-St.-Exupéry III
Marquis-d'Alesme Becker III
Marquis-de-Terme IV
Palmer III
Pouget IV
Prieuré IV
Rausan-Segla II
Rauzan-Gassies II
Du Tertre V

ST. JULIEN

Château
Belgrave V
Beychevelle IV
Branaire-Ducru IV
Camensac V
Ducru-Beaucaillou II
Gruaud-Larose II
Lagrange III
Langoa-Barton II

Château
La-Tour-Carnet IV
Léoville-Barton II
Léoville-Las-Cases II
Léoville-Poyferre II
St. Pierre-Bontemps IV
St. Pierre-Sevaistre IV
Talbot IV

PAUILLAC

Château
Lafite I
Latour I
Mouton-Rothschild II
Batailley V
Calvé-Croizet-Bages V
Clerc-Milon-Mondon V
Duhart-Milon IV
Grand-Puy-Ducasse V
Grand-Puy-Lacoste V
Haut-Bages-Libéral V

Château
Haut-Batailley V
Lynch-Bages V
Lynch-Moussas V
Pédesclaux V
Pichon-Longueville II
Pichon-Longueville-Lalande
II
Pontet-Canet V
Mouton-d'Armailhacq V

ST. ESTEPHE

Château
Calon-Ségur III
Cos-d'Estournel II
Cos Labory V

Château
Montrose II
Rochet IV

ST. ÉMILION

Château
Ausone
Cheval-Blanc
Beauséjour-Duffau-
Lagarosse
Beauséjour-Fagouet
Belair
Canon

Château
Figeac
Clos Fourtet
Gaffelière-Naudes
Magdelaine
Pavie
Trottevieille

P O M E R O L

Château
 Petrus
 l'Évangile
 Gazin
 La Conseillante
 Lafleur
 Lafleur-Petrus

Château
 Latour-Pomerol
 Nénin
 Petit-Village
 Trotanoy
 Vieux-Château-Certan

G R A V E S

Château
 Haut-Brion
 Domaine de Chevalier
 Haut-Bailly
 La Mission-Haut-Brion
 La Tour-Haut-Brion
 Latour-Martillac
 Pape-Clément

Château
 Bouscaut
 Carbonnieux
 Fieuzal
 Malartic-Lagravière
 Olivier
 Smith-Haut-Lafitte

G R A V E S   W H I T E S *

Château
 Bouscaut
 Carbonnieux
 Chevalier
 Couhins

Château
 Laville-Haut-Brion
 La Tour-Martillac
 Malartic-Lagravière
 Olivier

* Serve with fish, delicatessen.

SAUTERNES AND BARSAC*

Château	Château
D'Yquem	d'Arche
Bayle (Guiraud)	Broustet
Climens	Caillou
Coutet	Doisy
Peyraguey	Filhot
Rabaud	Lamothe
Rieussec	de Malle
de Suduiraut	de Myrat
La Tour-Blanche	Nairac
Vigneau	Romer
	Suau

* Serve with desserts.

Bouquet

This seemingly prissy word has a precise meaning in the short-hand which is wine language, indicating the collection of smells released when air comes in contact with a wine. These volatiles are primarily alcohols, each with its own fruity scent. The *original bouquet* is the smell of a newly made wine, the aroma, while the *bouquet acquit*, the "acquired bouquet," is the smell of a wine when it has reached maturity, the alcohols having slowly reacted to the fruit acids to produce esters. A *bouqueté* wine is one that has a big, full bouquet because it was initially high in fruit acid; Rhônes, Bordeaux wines of the Médoc, Burgundies of the Côte de Nuits, Rhine wines of the Rheingau and Palatinate, are particularly noted for their full bouquets.

Bourgeois [boor-zhwah]

Name applied to secondary vineyards of the Médoc, coming in quality right after the *Crus Classés*, or Classed Growths, and the Exceptional Growths. Many of them are château-bottled, and these are generally sound, inexpensive reds. Those called *Crus Bourgeois Supérieurs,* Superior Bourgeois Growths, are rated higher than those simply called *Crus Bourgeois.*

Bourgeuil [boor-zheuy]
Fruity red wines from the small Touraine district on the Loire, especially good with stews and meats with rich sauces.

Bourgogne [boor-gohn-yuh]
This means much more than merely the French word for Burgundy when it appears on a wine label. The designation is used to indicate merely that the wine comes from that region, if the phrase "Appellation d'Origine," or "Appellation Contrôlée," appears on the label. If the identifying phrase is "Bourgogne Supérieur," the wine contains an additional ½ per cent of alcohol, and is considered slightly better than "Bourgogne." Neither would be as good as a Burgundy from a specific district, township, or vineyard. Under the control laws, a wine bears the most specific name it is entitled to. The more specific the name, generally, the better the wine. Note, however, that the wines of Southern Burgundy, from the districts of Beaujolais, Mâconnais, and Chalonnais, are customarily marketed under the names of townships, while the best wines from Burgundy's heart, the Côte d'Or, are marketed under vineyard names, the township name not being enough to ensure a fine wine.

Bouzy [boo-zee]
Champagne district producing top wines from the Pinot Noir.

Brauneberg [*brow*-neh-bairg]
Once the most famous of the Mosel townships, it still produces some of the fullest of the Mosel wines, particularly good with pike or smoked salmon, ham or sausages.

Brouilly [brwee-yee]
A tongue-twister for Americans, this liquid name for one of the Beaujolais townships stands for fruity reds, at their best

when less than thirty months old, excellent with grillades or roast meats or fowl.

Brut [brü]
Term for the driest of Champagnes, to which little or no sweetening has been added. Almost parching in flavor, it is too dry for most tastes. It is usually the best Champagne of any particular house, because flaws in the wine cannot be hidden under sweetness. It is also the most expensive. Too dry for most foods, except possibly caviar, smoked turkey, *foie gras*, and the like, it is most frequently drunk by itself.

Burgundy
The French wine region that produces the greatest full, dry red and white table wines in the world, particularly the dry whites from the district of Chablis, the full-bodied reds from the Côte de Nuits, and the soft, rounded reds and full, dry whites from the Côte de Beaune, these last two districts comprising the fabled Côte d'Or. Southern Burgundy produces exceptional dry whites from the Pouilly-Fuissé district, and quickly maturing fruity reds from the districts of Beaujolais, Mâconnais, and Chalonnais. Those classed as Great Growths are listed in italics, and those considered to be *têtes de cuvées*, head vats, or best of the First Growths, are listed in roman. There are many other First Growths, identified by the phrase, *Premier Cru*, on the label. The finest Burgundies are always estate-bottled; that is, put in bottle at the vineyard by the grower. Wines from the lesser townships of the Côte de Beaune and Southern Burgundy are not necessarily estate-bottled, nor need they carry vineyard names, as should all first-rate wines from Chablis, the Côte de Nuits, and the major towns of the Côte de Beaune.

CÔTE DE NUITS REDS*

FIXIN

La Perrière
Les Hervelets

Le Clos du Chapitre
Les Arvelets

GEVREY-CHAMBERTIN

Le Chambertin
Chambertin-Clos de Bèze
Clos St. Jacques
Les Veroilles

Chapelle-Chambertin
Griotte-Chambertin
Latricières-Chambertin
Mazis-Chambertin
Mazoyères or
   Charmes-Chambertin
Ruchottes-Chambertin

MOREY-ST.-DENIS

Clos de la Roche
Clos St. Denis
Bonnes Mares

Clos de Tart
Clos de Lambrays
Le Clos Sorbés

CHAMBOLLE-MUSIGNY

Musigny
Bonnes Mares

Les Amoureuses
Les Charmes

VOUGEOT

Clos de Vougeot

FLAGEY-ÉCHÉZEAUX

Grands-Échézeaux

Échézeaux

* Wines set in italics are from superior vineyards.

VOSNE-ROMANÉE

Romanée-Conti   La Tâche
Romanée-St. Vivant   Richebourg
La Romanée

NUITS-ST.-GEORGES

Les St.-Georges   Les Cailles
Les Vaucrains   Les Porrets

CÔTE DE BEAUNE REDS

PRÉMEAUX

Clos des Corvées   Clos de la Maréchale
Clos des Forêts   Les Didiers

ALOXE-CORTON

Corton   Clos du Roi

PERNAND-VERGELESSES

Île des Vergelesses

SAVIGNY-LES-BEAUNE

Les Jarrons   Aux Vergelesses

BEAUNE

Les Bressandes   Les Fèves
Champs-Pimont   Les Grèves
Clos de la Mousse   Les Marconnets
Clos des Mouches

18

POMMARD

Les Rugiens-Bas
Les Rugiens-Hauts

Les Epenots
Les Petits-Epenots

VOLNAY

En Caillerets
Caillerets-Dessus
En Champans

En Chevret
Les Cras
Les Santenots
Les Petures

MEURSAULT

Clos de la Perrière
Les Perrières

Les Santenots
Les Cras
Les Petures

MONTHÉLIE

Les Champs-Fulliot

La Taupine

AUXEY-DURESSES

Les Bretterins

Les Duresses

CHASSAGNE-MONTRACHET

Clos St.-Jean
Morgeot

La Boudriotte

SANTENAY

Les Gravières

BURGUNDY WHITES

CHABLIS

Vaudesir
Les Preuses
Les Clos
Grenouilles
Bougros
Valmur
Blanchots

Montée de Tonnerre
Fourchaume
Vaillon
Beugnon
Les Forêts
Montmain
Côte de Léchet
Vaulorent
Mont de Mileu

ALOXE - CORTON

Corton Charlemagne

MEURSAULT

Perrières or Clos des Perrières
Les Genevrières

Les Charmes
Blagny

PULIGNY

Le Montrachet
Chevalier-Montrachet
Bâtard-Montrachet

Bienvenues-Bâtard-
Montrachet
Criots-Bâtard-Montrachet

CHASSAGNE

Bâtard-Montrachet
Morgeot

Les Grandes Ruchottes

CÔTE DE BEAUNE-VILLAGES

Pernand-Vergelesses
Ladoix-Serigny
Savigny-les-Beaune
Beaune
Monthélie

Auxey-Duresses
Blagny
St.-Aubin
Santenay

Cabernet [kah-bair-nay]
Cabernet Sauvignon is the complete name for this great red wine grape, or noble vine, of Bordeaux. This grape is always meant when the single word is used, although a close and good cousin is the Cabernet Franc, which is widely planted in St. Emilion and on the Loire. The Sauvignon is the informing vine of Bordeaux, meaning the one that sets the character of the wines; it also produces well in Napa, Sonoma, and Santa Clara Counties in California.

Cabinet
Special reserves of wine. See *Kabinettwein*.

California
The state produces about 90 per cent of our wines, nearly three fourths of which are cheap and sweet fortified wines from the Central Valley and Southern California. But in the so-called North Coast counties around San Francisco (Contra Costa and the valleys of Napa, Sonoma, and Livermore) excellent red, white, and pink wines are made, particularly those called *varietals*, marketed under the European grape names from which they are produced. Even there, however, many wines are made that are blends of secondary grapes, marketed under such European geographical names as Burgundy, Chablis, Rhine wine, Sauterne, Champagne, and so on. Others are called Mountain Red or White, or are named after the valleys from which they come. These blends are called standard wines, and are often good buys when the price is low; reds are generally better than whites.

Canada
Some good wines from hybrid and native grapes are produced on the Niagara Peninsula, occasionally comparing favorably to the standard wines of New York and California.

Canary
Wine from the Canary Islands in the Atlantic were popular in Elizabethan England, but the vineyards were mostly destroyed and only a little is now made for South American markets.

Cantenac [kahn-tuh-nak]
Town in the Médoc of Bordeaux, whose wines are marketed under the name of its neighbor, Margaux.

Cape wines
English term for South African wines.

Capri [*kah*-pree]
Good dry white wines from the mainland near Capri, the island itself, and the neighboring isle of Ischia, which produces the best, excellent with fish, sea food, *pasta*, ham, pork, and veal preparations.

Carafe [kah-raf]
Carafe wines are *vins ordinaires*, drawn from the cask in the restaurant and served in glass flasks.

Carema [kah-*reh*-mah]
Piedmont town producing fruity, full wines from the Nebbiolo grape, good with stews and roasts.

Cassis [kah-sees]
Town near Marseille producing dry whites and light *rosés*, good
with fish and sea food. A currant syrup called *crème de cassis*
is produced in Dijon, an ounce or two of which is added to
iced dry white Burgundies or dry Vermouths to make a quench-
ing apéritif. Soda water is often added.

Castelli di Jesi [kah-*stel*-lee dee yay-*see*]
Dry white from the Marches, near the Italian Adriatic, flowery
but with an occasional earth taste, the best known being
Verdicchio, excellent with fish or sea food, or ham.

Castelli Romani [kah-*stel*-lee ro-*mah*-ni]
Wines from the Alban hills near Rome, red or white, from such
towns as Albano, Frascati, Colonna, Marino, and Velletri. The
best are white, excellent with fish, sea food, *pasta*, ham and
pork dishes.

Catawba
Native American grape producing fair, spicy whites in New
York.

Chablis [shah-blee]
Famous full, dry whites from this tiny Burgundian district are
rare because of the harsh frosts in the spring. Three or four
times a decade, the vineyards are frozen so that little or no
wine is produced, as happened in 1959. The name has been
borrowed to use for mediocre standard wines produced in
California, New York, Australia, South Africa, and elsewhere;
the name has meaning only on authentic wines from the district. Seven vineyards are entitled to the appellation *Chablis
Grand Cru:*

Blanchots	Les Preuses
Bougros	Valmur
Les Clos	Vaudésir
Grenouille	

Less than two dozen vineyards are entitled to be called *Premiers
Crus* and are listed under "Burgundy." Others are called "Petit

Chablis" and "Chablis Villages," blends of wines from lesser vineyards, slightly better, perhaps, than those simply marketed as "Chablis." All are produced from the Pinot Chardonnay, generally reach their peak two years after the vintage, and are past their prime when six or seven years old. Chablis is the classic wine with oysters, and excellent with fish, sea food, ham and pork dishes.

Chalonnais [sha-lohn-nay]
One of the three districts of Southern Burgundy—the other two are Beaujolais and Mâconnais, from which comes Pouilly-Fuissé—whose vineyards extend for a dozen miles just below the Côte d'Or. The four townships included in the *Appellation d'Origine* laws are Rully, which produces small red wines; Mercurey, which produces a light, fruity red; Givry which produces a still lighter red; and Montagny, which produces a small white wine. Mercurey and Givry are pleasant luncheon wines, to serve with veal, fowl, or cold meat.

Chambertin [shahm-bair-tan]
Le Chambertin is one of the world's greatest red wines, a full, red Côte de Nuits Burgundy noted for its balance and bouquet. Its neighboring vineyard, Clos de Bèze, and seven adjoining vineyards, are entitled to use the word "Chambertin" on labels; these are listed, along with the First Growths of the township, under "Burgundy." The wines take four or five years to mature in good years, another year or so in great vintages, and often last for twenty years. Magnificent with roasts of beef or game, with roast fowl, and grillades or terrines.

Chambéry [sham-bay-ree]
Town in the French Savoy noted for dry vermouth.

Chambolle-Musigny [sham-bol-mü-zee-nyee]
Town of Burgundy's Côte de Nuits celebrated for its delicate, balanced red wines with very flowery bouquets, the Great Growths being Le Musigny and Bonnes Mares; First Growths are listed under "Burgundy." Superb wines with fowl, particularly small game birds, with steaks and roasts, particularly beef.

Chambrée [shahm-bray]

A chambered wine originally meant one that was removed from a cool wine cellar, opened, and then allowed to warm slowly to the temperature of the room in which it was going to be served. But rooms were much cooler in the old days, so that to warm, or *chambrer*, a red wine today means to let it warm slowly to a temperature between 65 and 75 degrees, so that it is still cool to the lips. This does not mean heating the wine.

Champagne

The great white sparkling wine from the region east of Paris has had its name stolen by lesser sparkling wines made elsewhere in the world. The true Champagne is always fermented in the bottle, the carbon dioxide released by secondary fermentations being caught with the wine, so the bubble, or bead, is closely bound to the wine itself. Champagnes are usually blended in vats before bottling, the batch being called a *cuvée*, the wine coming from both Pinot Noir and Pinot Chardonnay grapes. A vintage Champagne is a blend of wines from a single year, but nonvintage Champagnes may be from several vintages; this blending is necessary to balance the wines for fullness, bouquet, and so forth, and is quite proper. Certain townships within the region have vineyards of exceptional quality, and are rated as 100 per cent vineyards; their wines are blended with those from vineyards rated 90 per cent and lower. Champagne made only from Pinot Noir is called *blanc de noirs*, and this "white of blacks" generally comes from the 100 per cent

vineyards of the Montagne de Reims towns of Verzenay, Mailly, and Bouzy, or the Marne towns of Ambonnay and Ay. Those made from the Pinot Chardonnay, *blanc de blancs*, generally come from Mesnil, Cramant, and Avize, towns strung along a ridge running south from Epernay, which is the capital of the region. Many of the wines are matured in deep cellars under the city of Reims. Champagnes take about six years to mature in bottle, and are sweetened with a dosage of sugar syrup before marketing, the cork being pulled, the sugar syrup being added, and the bottle being recorked quickly, so that little of the precious bubble escapes. *Brut* is the driest of Champagne types, none or less than 1 per cent sugar syrup being added. *Extra Sec* is the next driest, containing less than 3 per cent sugar; *Sec* contains up to 4 per cent, *Demi-Sec* up to 8 per cent, and *Doux*, or sweet, as much as 10 per cent. Brut is usually drunk by itself, without food, or perhaps with dry biscuits, smoked ham or turkey, *foie gras* or caviar. Extra Sec and Sec are very good with all foods, while sweet Champagnes are excellent with desserts. Champagnes can be served all through a meal, but generally taste best with delicate foods that have a distinctive flavor. They should be well chilled, but not icy.

Champagne de Cru [shahm-pan-yuh duh krü]
Vineyard Champagne, actually a *cuvée* made up of wines from a particular township, usually a *blanc de blancs* from Mesnil, Avise, or Cramant, and invariably a well-made Brut.

Chardonnay [shar-dohn-nay]
The great white wine grape, usually called Pinot Chardonnay, that produces all the great white Burgundies, and is also planted in the Champagne region, where it produces *blanc de blancs*. Some pleasant white wines are produced from this grape in California.

Charmat process [shar-mah]
Bulk-process method of making *sparkling wines*, which see.

Chassagne-Montrachet [shahs-sahn-yuh-mawn-rah-shay]
The southernmost major wine town of Burgundy's Côte d'Or,

producing fine, full whites, including part of the vineyards of Le Montrachet and Bâtard Montrachet, and several *Premiers Crus*, listed under Burgundy. Fine with fish and sea food, ham, pork, and veal dishes.

Chasselas [shas-suh-las]
The greatest French table, or eating, grape, used for wines in Pouilly-sur-Loire, the Gutedel of Germany, the Swiss Fendant.

Château [shah-to]
This word is used to identify individual vineyards in Bordeaux, where it precedes the vineyard name. It was originally used to indicate that the wines came from the castles of Bordeaux, and it is used elsewhere to give a royal cachet to the wines, although only a few non-Bordeaux wines are properly entitled to the name. The château wines are listed under Bordeaux.

Château-bottling
The system of bottling the wine at the vineyard by the owner, a sure way of identifying an authentic Bordeaux, if the vineyard is on the accepted lists.

Château-Chalon [shah-to-shah-lawn]
A Jura district dominated by an ancient castle, hence the name, identifying a pale yellow Sherry-like wine that is considered the finest of the Jura, takes six years to mature in cask, and lives for decades. It is always found in squat bottles that hold about 21 ounces. A fine apéritif wine, excellent with appetizers.

Château-Grillet [shah-to-gree-yay]
A great white wine, full-bodied and fruity, from the tiny Rhône district of Condrieu, just south of Lyon. Made from the Vionnier grape, it is superb with fish, crayfish and other sea food, served hot or cold, with all kinds of terrines, *pâtés*, and delicatessen.

Châteauneuf-du-Pape [shah-to-nuhf-dü-pap]
The Rhône district near Avignon famous for full, fruity red wines that take at least thirty months to mature, must contain

at least 12½ per cent alcohol, and are produced from a melange
of a dozen grapes. Some white wines and some *rosés* are made,
but most of the large production is the famous red wine. Many
of the vineyards use the word "château" with their name, not
so much to imitate Bordeaux, but more to pay tribute to that
French pope who made the district famous by building a new
summer château there in the Middle Ages. Excellent wines
with hearty dishes like stews and braised meats.

Chavignol [shah-veen-yohl]
Town in the Sancerre district of the upper Loire producing
very light whites and some *rosés*, best when less than three years
old, with fish, white meats, delicatessen.

Chénas [shay-nah]
Area near famous Moulin-à-Vent in the Beaujolais, producing similar full reds to serve with roasts and stews.

Chénin Blanc [shay-nan blahn]
White wine grape of the Loire, often called the Pineau de la
Loire because it is a variety of Burgundy's Pinot, and marketed
as the White Pinot in California. Wines are soft and flowery,
good with fish and sea food.

Chianti [kyahn-tee]
The famous red wine of Florence. The fruity young wines are
marketed in the round, straw-covered *fiasco*, but full, well-
balanced reds are marketed in Bordeaux bottles when five or
six years old. Sangiovese grapes are mostly used, with some

Canaiolo and Trebbiano; some ordinary whites are produced. Young Chiantis are at their best when under two years old, and are good with meats served with hearty sauces and stews, while the old Chiantis are good with roasts and grillades.

Chile
The best wines of South America, full, cheap whites from the Riesling being best when two or three years old, the equally cheap, full reds being more ordinary. Sold under ranch names like Undurraga, Vial, Santa Rita. The best region is Maipo, and the wines are good when sound, inexpensive bottles are needed to go with a casserole or buffet supper.

Chinon   [shee-nohn]
Delicious, fruity reds from this small Loire district are made from the Cabernet Franc grape of Bordeaux, and are excellent with chicken, white meat stews, and casseroles.

Cinque Terre   [cheen-kway tare-reh]
A white wine of the Italian Riviera, sometimes dry and flowery, but often slightly sweet. The dry is good with fish and sea food, the sweet by itself or with ham, sausages, and delicatessen.

Claret
The English name for the red wines of Bordeaux, not often used on wine labels, and deriving from the light-colored red wines called *clairette* that were shipped from Bordeaux centuries ago.

Classed Growth
Term used in the English-speaking world for the rated vineyards, *Crus Classés*, of *Bordeaux*, which see.

Climat   [klee-mah]
The French word for climate also means vineyard in Burgundy, where it implies conditions beyond soil, sun, and grape, such as exposure, drainage, frequency of mists, and other physical characteristics that affect the quality of the wines.

Clos [klo]
Originally this word meant a walled vineyard of good repute that had been enclosed to protect the vines; it is still used in Burgundy and elsewhere as a name for a vineyard, with or without walls.

Clos de Vougeot [klo duh voo-zho]
The Clos de Vougeot's 125 acres, comprising the largest in Burgundy's Côte d'Or, are now divided among more than forty proprietors. The wine is listed as a Grand Cru, but the best reds come from the upper third of the vineyard. Some full white wine, called Clos Blanc de Vougeot, is produced just outside the walls of the great vineyard. The reds are soft, full, and well-balanced, excellent with meat and game, roasts and grillades.

Collares [ko-*lar*-ehs]
Good, fruity Portuguese red wine produced near Lisbon, to be served with stews and hearty meat dishes.

Commanderia [ko-mahn-deh-*ree*-ah]
Full, rich, sweet red wine from Cyprus.

Condrieu [kohn-dree-eu]
Small Rhône district below Lyon famous for the great white Château-Grillet, best with fish or delicatessen.

Conegliano [ko-neh-*lyah*-no]
District north of Venice producing sweet white Prosecco, and the dry, flowery white Verdiso, the last being good with fish, ham, delicatessen, *pastas*.

Constantia
The best-known of the South African districts, producing good red and white wines, on a par with those from Paarl and Stellenbosch.

Contra Costa
County east of San Francisco which produces good red wines in its mountain vineyards, especially Gamay and Pinot Noir.

Corbières [kor-byair]
A full, coarse red wine, one of the best from the Midi, in southern France, excellent with hearty meat dishes.

Corked wine
A wine is said to be corky when it tastes of the cork, not the wine, a sign that the wine has gone bad.

Coronata [koh-ro-*nah*-tah]
Pale, delicate, fresh white wine from a town near Genoa, excellent with fish and *pastas*.

Corton [kor-tawn]
Great reds and whites (Corton and Corton Charlemagne) from the northernmost town of the Côte de Beaune, Aloxe-Corton, and from some of the vineyards of the neighboring Pernand-Vergelesses. The full, balanced reds are magnificent with roasts and grillades, the full-dry whites are superb with fish, ham, delicatessen.

Corvo [*kor*-vo]
Full, dry Sicilian white made partly from the Bordeaux grape, Sauvignon, excellent with fish, sea food, ham and pork products, *pastas*.

Coteaux de la Loire [ko-to duh lah lwahr]
Full and flowery, dry and slow to mature, wines from the banks of the Loire are outstanding in the Anjou, particularly those from the township of Savennières. High in alcohol, they take two years to mature, and are matchless with shad, crayfish, and other fruits of the sea.

Coteaux du Loir [ko-to dü lwahr]
Wines from vineyards on this Anjou tributary of the Loire (sweet whites, light fresh *rosés*, and thin reds) should not be confused with big, full whites from the Coteaux de la Loire, although they are generally served with the same sort of fish and luncheon dishes.

Côte de Beaune   [koht duh bohn]

Beaune slope—*côte* means flank or side or shore, as well—is the southern half of Burgundy's Côte d'Or, some twelve miles of vineyards extending from the township of Aloxe-Corton to below Chassagne-Montrachet, including the important towns of Beaune, Pommard, Volnay, and Puligny-Montrachet, as well as smaller and less-important communes like Pernand-Vergelesses, Savigny-les-Beaune, Auxey-Duresses, Blagny, and Santenay. The great red is Corton, although lighter, softer reds from Beaune, Pommard, and Volnay are famous. The great whites are Corton Charlemagne and Montrachet, although Meursault and Beaune whites are also famous. Vineyard names are important in the major towns, but are often dispensed with on labels of wines from the smaller communes, which in some cases are allowed to market wines with the names of the major towns. The reds are good with meats and fowl, the whites with pork products and *pâtés*, fish and sea food.

Côte de Nuits   [koht duh nwee]

The northern half of the Côte d'Or, twelve miles of vineyards that include the towns of Fixin, Gevrey-Chambertin, Morey-St.-Denis, Chambolle-Musigny, Clos Vougeot, Flagey-Échézeaux, Vosne-Romanée, and Nuits-St.-Georges. These full reds with their big bouquets are the classic wines for game and wild fowl of all kinds, with roasts and grillades, with fowl and other meats served with hearty sauces.

Côte d'Or   [koht dohr]

The heart of Burgundy, less than thirty miles of great vineyards, all of which are along a single range of hills, the best being located in the curve where the flat land meets the rise. The Slope of Gold has two parts, the northern Côte de Nuits producing full, well-balanced reds, the southern Côte de Beaune producing softer reds and full, dry whites. Nuits reds take three or four years to mature in a good year, another year or two in a great year, and unless the wines are very soft the wines will still be in their prime anywhere from a dozen years to two decades after the vintage. Beaune reds take two or three years to mature, live for a decade after that in great years, Corton and Pommard and Volnay reds lasting even longer. The great whites are ready two years after the vintage and are past their prime when eight years old, while the lesser whites should be drunk up within five years after the vintage. The Pinot Noir is used for all the great reds, the Pinot Chardonnay for all the great whites. Excellent with all hearty foods, and ones that are simply cooked but full of flavor, dishes of subtlety or delicacy generally being served with Bordeaux or other more delicate wines.

Côte-Rôtie [koht-ro-tee]

The fruitiest of all French red wines, and one of the finest, produced in the smal Rhône district just south of Lyon. The vineyards are steep and terraced, the northern half of the two-mile slope being called the Côte Brune, the southern half, producing lighter, softer wines, being called the Côte Blonde. The two are often blended. They often take six years and longer to develop, and many vintages live for two or three decades. These big, generous wines have a fruity taste of raspberries, which comes from the Syrah grape, and they are best with dishes that are served with a flavorsome sauce, and with such cold preparations as terrines and galantines; they are frequently served with chicken and beef dishes.

Côtes [koht]

Word often applied to minor districts, generally those on slopes or hillsides, partly in imitation of the Burgundian use of the word. Loosely, the word means a group of vineyards, whose

wines are often blended together. In the singular, the word is applied to vineyards on a single slope.

Côtes du Rhône [koht dü rohn]
There are red-wine vineyards in sections all along the Rhône, and these are blended to make a full red wine of big body that is inexpensive and always pleasant to drink with stews and other hearty meat dishes.

Coupage [koo-pahzh]
Blending, the technique of mixing lesser wines to mask defects, wines that are too light being blended with wines that are too heavy, those that are too acid with those that are too bland. The stated purpose is to make fair wines out of ones that are too out of balance to be palatable, but *coupage* is also used to increase the quantity of good wines with lesser, neutral ones. Regionals from any wine district are blends. The practice is necessary in so-called "made wines," those that are not the simple and natural product of a vineyard. Fortified wines and sparkling wines are invariably blended, the result nearly always being an improvement. It is only in districts of great table wines (Bordeaux, Burgundy, the Rhine vineyards) that *coupage* is considered reprehensible, where many fine and distinctive small wines from individual vineyards are dumped into the blending vats because their names are not famous enough to command a market. In table-wine regions, *coupage* is called the *grande cuisine*, great skill being needed to mix up acceptable batches; the result is generally ignored by those fond of table wines, although shippers argue that there is a good market for regional blends—standard wines that taste about the same from one year to the next—and not for the small vineyard wines with minor flaws.

Cramant [krah-mahn]
Township of the Champagne region with top-rated vineyards planted in the white Pinot Chardonnay, often bottled separately to produce *blanc de blancs*, light Champagne from white grapes, also called *Champagne de Cru.*

Crémant [kray-mahn]
A partly sparkling, or creaming, wine made in the Champagne region, excellent with ham and terrines.

Crème de tête [krem duh tet]
Name used for wines made from special sections of a vineyard, or from culled grapes, or selected butts of wine. Château d'Yquem used to produce this wine, but in 1921 decided to eliminate everything but the crème de tête from each vintage, so that today all of this great Sauternes could be so designated. The practice is no longer followed much in France.

Crescenz [kress-sentz]
Word used on a label to identify a wine that is estate-bottled, from a particular vineyard and put in bottle by the owner.

Crozes-Hermitage [krohz-air-mee-tahzh]
A district on the ridge behind the Rhône district of Hermitage, producing similar but less-good red wines that are served with roasts and stews.

Cru [krü]
The word means "growth" or vineyard, and implies classification. In France, foods of particular quality are classified into *crus*, among them the Marennes oysters, Macau artichokes, Bresse chickens, Périgord truffles, and even the Limousin oaks used to make casks for Cognac.

Crus Classés [krü klah-say]
Cru means growth or vineyard in French, and generally a classed growth is one that is included on the official lists of the *Appellations d'Origine* drawn up for each French district, but more specifically the classed growths are those of Bordeaux; the five numbered growths, followed by the Exceptional Growths, the Superior Burgeois Growths, and the *Crus Bourgeois, Artisan*, and *Paysan*, which are generally used for blends. These growths are in the Médoc. There are two numbered growths of Sauternes. Official lists of Graves, St. Emilion, and Pomerol are now considered as classified growths, by extension.

Crusted Port

Perhaps the greatest type of Port, bottled within three years of the vintage and then shipped to the country where it is to be drunk, where it ripens in the bottle for ten to twenty years, forming a hard crust in the bottle. England gets almost all the Crusted Port, where it is drunk after a meal, with cheese, nuts, and fruit.

Cuvée [kü-vay]

From the word *cuve*, meaning vat, a term applied to each particular blend of wines in Champagne, and in Burgundy to the wines from individual vineyards that are sold at auction by the Hospices de Beaune under the names of the donors; these are among the best wines of the Côte de Beaune, but generally high in price.

Decanting

Wines continue to develop in the bottle, and while wines that are meant to be drunk within five years of the bottling are so thoroughly filtered that they cast little sediment, those that mature in bottle for a longer period will throw a deposit. In most cases, this simply indicates that the wine should be handled carefully and poured slowly. Sediment doesn't impair the qualities of a wine, on the contrary indicating that the wine has developed, but the sediment is unpleasant to taste. If there is much deposit in the bottle, the wine is brought from the cellar the day before and stood up so that all sediment will settle. The wine is then poured off into another bottle or decanter so that the sediment is left behind, the pouring being stopped when the first particles of sediment begin to move out of the neck of the bottle. This decanting is done with a continuous pour, so that the wine won't flow back to rouse the settled deposit. It is customary to set the decanted bottle near the container of poured-out wine so that the drinkers can see what they will be drinking. In Europe, the steward may whisper to each guest the name and vintage of the wine as he pours, instead of showing the bottle, or the host may announce the wine, but this is quite formal service. Decanting a wine that does not need decanting is considered pretentious, except where the hostess may delight in showing a decanter.

Deidesheim [*dy*-des-hime]
The greatest town of the Rheinpfalz (see), and the home of many fine growers; there are over 500 acres of Riesling, producing great Deidesheimers from Hohenmorgen, Kieselberg, Leinhöhle, and many others, excellent with fish, sea food, and delicatessen.

Delaware
The best of the native white-wine grapes producing good wines in Finger Lakes vineyards of New York, in Ohio, and on Canada's Niagara Peninsula, good when young with fish, ham, and delicatessen.

Dhron [drohn]
Town of the Mittel-Mosel producing some good Rieslings to serve with fish or delicatessen.

Dienheim [*deen*-hime]
Town of the Rheinhessen next to Oppenheim that produces some good Rieslings to serve with fish, delicatessen.

Dom Perignon [dohm peh-reen-yawn]
A monk and cellar-master in Champagne at the beginning of the eighteenth century who is credited with first using corks instead of waxed cloth to seal wine bottles, which enabled him to invent Champagne, by trapping the bubbles.

Dosage [do-sahzh]
Name for the amount of sweet syrup or brandy added to some wines.

Douro [*Doo*-ro]
The river and district in northern Portugal of the Port vine-yards, although most of the wine is matured in lodges across from Oporto, the city at the river's mouth.

Doux [doo]
The French word for sweet, applied to sweet Champagne, and to V.D.N., *vin doux naturel*, sweet dessert wines produced mainly near the Spanish border in the towns of Banyuls, Fron-tignan, Agly, Rousillon, Rivesaltes, and Maury, particularly those produced from Muscat grapes.

Dry
In wine parlance, the absence of sweetness; sourness is not implied at all, a sour wine being a wine gone bad. A dry wine generally has a tart, lively quality, derived from its fruit acids, that is often sharp and biting in ordinary wines.

Durkheim [*doork*-hime]
The main town of the Rheinpfalz, producing much ordinary red wine and some good Rieslings, the best-known vineyards being Spielberg and Michelsberg; good with fish.

Eau-de-vie [o-duh-vee]
The French term for distilled spirits.

Échézeaux [esh-ay-zo]
One of the greatest wines of Burgundy's Côte de Nuits, whose full, balanced reds from vineyards in the town of Flagey-Échézeaux go to market under this name, and with the prefix *Grands*. Superb wines with roasts and grillades, with game and wildfowl.

Edelfaule [*aid*-uhl-fow-luh]
German word for noble mold. See *Auslese*.

Edelzwicker [*aid*-uhl-tsvik-uhr]
Name for a blend of Alsatian white wines, good with fish and delicatessen.

Egri Bikaver [*egg*-ree *bee*-cah-ver]
A full red wine of good quality from the Eger district of Hungary, made from the Bikaver grape, which means bull's blood. The dark red wine is good with stews and hearty meat dishes.

Eitelsbach [*eye*-tuls-bok]
A township of the Ruwer famous for its light and delicate wines—excellent with fish and delicatessen—from vineyards around the Carthusian monastery of Karthäuserhofberg, on some of which a tiny label is used as contrast to the long name.

Eltville [*elt*-feel]
A large town of the Rheingau producing medium-priced soft and flowery wines from a long hillside above the river. Among the best-known vineyards are Sonnenberg and Langenstück. Excellent luncheon wines with delicatessen, fish, and sea food.

Elvira
Native American grape grown in New York that produces ordinary white wines.

Enkirch [*en*-keerk]
Town of the Mittel-Mosel producing delicate wines, often excellent in great years, to serve with fish, sea food.

Entre-Deux-Mers [on-truh-duh-mair]
A secondary Bordeaux district producing ordinary wines.

Erbach [*air*-bok]
Rheingau township famous for its Marcobrunn, a vineyard producing full, fruity, superbly balanced whites. Other Erbachers, from such vineyards as Siegelsberg and Steinmorgen, are harder but equally long-lived. Excellent with all sorts of fish and delicatessen.

Erden [*air*-den]

The vineyards of this famous Mosel township are extremely steep and terraced, and produce superbly full wines even in poor years. Top vineyards include Treppchen, Prälat. Erdeners are excellent with fish and delicatessen.

Est! Est!! Est!!!

A pleasant Italian white wine from Muscat grapes produced near Montefiascone named in honor of a German bishop on the road to Rome who was said to have sent his servant on ahead to taste the wines, then chalk comment on the tavern wall. He was carried away by this wine, and overchalked; the bishop overdrank and died. The story is overtold and the wine is overrated.

Estate-bottled

Term for a wine that is bottled at the vineyard by the owner, a mark of superior quality in Burgundy, Germany, and elsewhere, equivalent to the château-bottling system of Bordeaux.

Etna

Red wines from the slope of that volcano, good with *pastas* and hearty meat dishes.

Falerno [fah-*lehr*-no]

Falernian was a famous ancient wine from vineyards in the Naples countryside, today producing only ordinary reds and whites.

Falernum

A sweetening syrup of the West Indies made from limes and almonds.

Feuillette [feu-yet]

Burgundian name for a half-cask that contains about 144 bottles of wine, used particularly in places where production is small, as in Chablis.

Fillette [fee-yet]

The French for little girl, used in the Touraine to name a half-bottle.

Filtering
Because people have an inordinate aversion to sediment, wines are much more heavily filtered today than formerly, to the detriment of the wine. Fine screens of asbestos and other materials are used to remove particles in suspension.

Fine Champagne   [feen shahm-pahn-yuh]
Often called *Grande Fine Champagne*, this is an expensive blend of well-aged Cognacs from the two best vineyard sections, called Grande Champagne and Petite Champagne, the first being heavy and slow-aging, the second being less fine, less pungent, and quick to age. The blend is better than either one alone, and tastes best when sipped slowly and allowed to trickle down the throat.

Finesse   [fee-ness]
A precise term used to identify a quality of the greatest wines of Bordeaux, Burgundy, Champagne, and the Rhine, denoting a combination of delicacy and strength, a balance of characteristics in a wine that is superlatively just what it is supposed to be, without flaw. It is almost untranslatable, but easy to recognize.

Finger Lakes
The best wine-producing area of the East, centering around Keuka and Canandaigua Lakes in upper New York State. America's best sparkling wines are produced here, along with ʒood whites from the Delaware grape, and hybrids.

Fining
Technique of clearing wine by letting a froth of egg whites or other thick liquid sink through it, as a liquid net that catches suspended solids and drags them to the bottom of the cask. After fining, the wine is drawn off the residue, called the *lees*.

Finish
The aftertaste or end taste of a wine or spirit, which should be a continuation of the taste, not something quite different.

Fino [*fee*-no]
The lightest, palest, and youngest of the three main types of Spanish Sherry (see), excellent with delicatessen and spicy foods. Should be chilled.

First Growths
The best vineyards of a township, except for an occasional one that is called a Great Growth. *Premier Cru* is an official term in France, but only has this precise meaning when the *Appellation Contrôlée* phrase appears on the bottle.

Fixin [fee-san]
The northernmost town of the Côte de Nuits, producing outstanding, full, balanced red wines magnificent with meats, fowl and game, particularly from La Perrière and Clos du Chapitre.

Flagey-Échézeaux
See *Échézeaux*.

Fleurie
See *Beaujolais*.

Flor
The flower, or yeast, that forms on the top of Spanish Sherries of the Fino type, which accounts for their unique taste.

Flowery
A flowery wine is a young wine that has the fresh taste and smell of flowers—no one in particular. This changes in an old wine to more subtle qualities called *bouquet*. Young reds, like Beaujolais, and the white wines are noted for floweriness, par-

ticularly the Rieslings and Sylvaners made from those grapes in the Rhine vineyards.

Folle Blanche   [fol blahnsh]
White wine grape that produces the acid wine from which Cognac is made, but producing a good, fresh white wine in the North Coast counties of California.

Forst
Ranking with Deidesheim as the outstanding wine-producing town of the Palatinate, its more than 300 acres of Rieslings include Jesuitengarten and Kirchenstück, the most valuable vineyard land in Germany, noted for outstanding bouquet, balance, and finesse. The Forsters are magnificent full wines to serve with veal, ham, and other pork products, with fish and sea food.

Fortified wine
One of the major kinds of wine, to which brandy has been added to hold the wine to a desired taste. The great fortified wines are the Sherries of Spain and the Ports of Portugal, while Madeira from that Atlantic island is often added to form a trinity. Often-excellent fortified wines are made in Malaga, while good wines are produced on Sicily, called Marsala, and some good Muscat wines are made in southern France near the Spanish border. Imitations made elsewhere in the world do not compare.

Foxiness
A musky tang recognizable in native grapes, most particularly in the Concord and the Catawba. When slight, this taste is pleasing; when heavy, it is not, and must be disguised under sweetness.

Fraise   [frehz]
The white *eau de vie* made from strawberries; the best comes from Alsace, is aged in crocks, is very rare and expensive, and is often chilled, then allowed to warm as it is slowly sipped. Served after meals.

Framboise [fram-bwahz]
The white *eau de vie* made from raspberries; the best comes
from Alsace, is expensive, and is sipped slowly, after meals.
Sometimes chilled.

France
The greatest wine country on earth, producing one and a half
billion gallons a year, most of which is ordinary. Great wines
come from Bordeaux, Burgundy, Champagne; good ones from
the Rhône, Loire, Alsace, and elsewhere. See these.

Franconia
Region in the valley of the Main River, noted for fresh white
wines shipped in flask-shaped bottles, and called *Frankenwein,*
or *Steinwein,* after the most important vineyard of the region,
the Würzburger Stein. Generally blends from Riesling, Sylvaner, and Traminer grapes, these good luncheon wines go
well with fish and delicatessen.

Franken Riesling [*fran*-ken *rees*-ling]
Name for the Sylvaner in Germany, an almost disparaging
term, often used without the first name in California, where
the true Riesling is called Johannisberg Riesling.

Frascati [frah-*skah*-tee]
Good white wine from the Castelli Romani, popular in Rome
with *pasta* and spiced meats.

Freisa [*fray*-zuh]
Fruity red grape, producing a sometimes slightly sparkling red
wine of Italy's Piedmont, good with stews; called freezha in
California, where it does well.

Frontignan [fron-teen-yahn]
Good sweet dessert wine from the Muscat grape from the French district near the Spanish border.

Fruitiness
The juicy quality of wines that have the taste of fruit, which changes to more subtle taste in old wines. Particularly notable in Beaujolais reds, and the full whites of the Rheinpfalz or the Rheingau.

Fuder [*foo*-der]
The name for the big German wine casks used on the Mosel, which contain 1,000 liters, or 265 gallons, or the equivalent of about 110 cases of 12 bottles each. The wine is often sold cask by cask.

Full
A wine term that expresses the opposite of thin or bland or watery. In reference to body, fullness implies a taste with no hint of wateriness; with reference to bouquet, it suggests a wine with heavy aromas rather than light ones, or the presence of them rather than their absence.

Furmint [*fur*-mint]
The golden Hungarian grape used in Tokay vineyards.

Gamay [ga-may]
Grape used for Beaujolais, excellent and fruity when young, but producing secondary wines elsewhere in Burgundy and good, young wines in California.

Geisenheim [*gize*-en-hime]
Rheingau township producing good, full wines in ordinary years, great *Auslesen* in fine years. Outstanding vineyards include Rothenberg and Mäuerchen, excellent with fish, ham, and delicatessen.

Gentil [zhon-tee]
Blend of Alsatian white wines marketed as Edelzwicker, good with delicatessen.

Germany

All of Germany's fine wines are white, great ones from the Rhineland districts of the Rheinpfalz, Rheinhessen, Rheingau, and the Mosel, made from the Riesling grape, and good wines made from the Sylvaner and Traminer grapes planted in the Rheinpfalz, Rheinhessen, Franconia, and Baden. The best wines are estate-bottled with the name of the vineyard and grower on the label. They are excellent wines to drink by themselves, in place of cocktails, highballs, or beer, and with various luncheon, buffet, or light dishes, including all kinds of fish and sea food, simply cooked fowl and pork, or hams, cheeses, and delicatessen. Representative vineyards are listed by township:

T H E   M O S E L L E

E R D E N	G R A A C H
Treppchen	Josephshofer
Prälat	Himmelreich
U R Z I G	B E R N K A S T E L
Würzgarten	Doktor
Schwarzlay	Lay
Z E L T I N G E N	B R A U N E B E R G
Himmelreich	Juffer
Schlossberg	Falkenberg
W E H L E N	P I E S P O R T
Sonnenuhr	Goldtröpfchen
Nonnenberg	Lay

THE SAAR

WILTINGEN
Scharzhofberg
Scharzberg

OBEREMMEL
Hütte
Agritiusberg

AYL
Kupp
Herrenberg

OCKFEN
Bockstein
Geisberg

KANZEM
Altenberg
Sonnenberg

NEIDERMEN-NIG
Euchariusberg

SERRIG
Schloss
Saarfelser
Vogelsang

THE RUWER

MAXIMIN GRUNHAUS
Herrenberg

KASEL
Nieschen
Taubenberg

EITELSBACH
Karthäuserhofberger

TRIER

AVELSBACH

47

THE RHEINPFALZ

W A C H E N H E I M
Goldbächel
Gerümpel

F O R S T
Jesuitengarten
Kirchenstück

D E I D E S H E I M
Hohenmorgen
Leinhöhle

**R U P P E R T S -
B E R G**
Gaisböhl
Spiess

K Ö N I G S B A C H
Bender
Harle

**B A D
D U R K H E I M**

U N G S T E I N

K A L L S T A D T

THE RHEINHESSEN

N A C K E N H E I M
Rothenberg
Engelsberg

N I E R S T E I N
Rehbach
Hipping

O P P E N H E I M
Kreuz
Sackträger

B I N G E N
Scharlachberg
Ohligberg

D I E N H E I M
Goldberg
Krotenbrunnen

W O R M S

B O D E N H E I M

HOCHHEIM
Domdechaney
Kirchenstück

ELTVILLE
Sonnenberg
Langenstück

RAUENTHAL
Baiken
Gehrn

KIEDRICH
Gräfenberg
Wasserrose

ERBACH
Marcobrunner
Siegelsberg

HATTENHEIM
Steinberger
Wisselbrunnen

OESTRICH
Lenchen
Doosberg

HALLGARTEN
Schönhell
Mehrhölzchen

WINKEL
Schloss Vollrads
Hasensprung

JOHANNIS-BERG
Schloss Johannisberg
Klaus

GEISENHEIM
Rothenberg
Mäuerchen

RUDESHEIM
Berg Rottland
Berg Roseneck

Gevrey-Chambertin [zhev-ray-shahm-bair-tan]
Township of Burgundy's Côte de Nuits which includes all ten of the great vineyards legally allowed to add Chambertin to their names, plus several others almost as good. Reds simply bearing the town name can be good but often are not. The

great estate-bottled reds are noted for fullness, balance, and bouquet, perfect wines with prime meats and fowl, game and wildfowl, terrines and *pâtés*, and fine cheeses.

Gewürztraminer [guh-vürts-trah-*mee*-ner]
Often excellent white wine from the grape of that name, best from Alsace and Rheinhessen; good with sausages and other delicatessen.

Gigondas [zhee-gohn-dahs]
Good, full red wine of the Rhône to serve with stews, steaks.

Giro [*jee*-ro]
Good red dessert wine of Sardinia.

Good wines
A good wine is one that tastes good, goes the standard definition, but a more precise one is that the wine does not develop much once it is bottled. It should be characteristic of the grape and district, with a well-rounded bouquet and a winy and not watery taste, in balance with its other qualities. Most good wines develop in cask in two years or less, although red wines of the Rhône and Italy often take twice as long and longer. Good red wines can live three or four years in bottle, and even longer, but are best within a year or two of being bottled. Good white wines should be drunk as soon as they are available, and are past their prime five years after the vintage, often sooner.

Graach [grok]
One of the greatest Mosel townships, producing beautifully balanced full white wines from such vineyards as Himmelreich and Domprobst. Graachers are magnificent with delicate fish, ham and pork products.

Gragnano [gron-*yah*-no]
Good fruity Italian red wine from this Campania district is excellent with hearty stews, roasts, and cheeses.

Grand vin [gron van]
This is a term very loosely applied in France to almost any wine.

Grape
Wine grapes are quite different from table, or eating, grapes, and all good ones are of the species *Vitis vinifera*. Those producing the great table wines, the "noble vines," are Burgundy's *Pinot Noir* and the Bordeaux *Cabernet* and *Merlot*; good ones are the *Gamay* of Beaujolais, the *Nebbiolo* of the Italian Piedmont, and the *Syrah* of the Rhône. The noble vines for white table wines are the *Pinot Chardonnay* of Burgundy and Champagne, the *Sauvignon* and *Semillon* of Bordeaux, and the German *Riesling*, while good ones include the *Sylvaner*, *Traminer*, and *Gewürztraminer* of the Rhineland, and the *Chénin Blanc* of the Loire. The *Grenache* produces the best pink wines.

Graves [grahv]
One of the great districts of Bordeaux, producing magnificent light, balanced reds, and some good, flowery whites. See *Bordeaux*.

Gray Riesling
California euphemism for the Chauché Gris grape.

Great wine
The classic definition is that a great wine be long-lived and typical of the grape and district from which it comes, which is another way of saying that it should live long enough to develop subtle secondary characteristics during its time in bottle, often as much as ten years for the great Bordeaux, Burgundy, and Rhône reds, as little as two years for the great dry Burgundy whites like Montrachet, Corton, and Chablis, or the Rieslings

from the Rhineland. Champagne may take six years from the vintage to be ready to drink, while fortified wines like Sherry, Port, and Marsala need ten or more. Sweet wines like Sauternes, Tokay, and the *Auslesen* from Rhineland vineyards need two or three years in bottle.

Greece
Good table wines come from the districts of Dekeleia, Achaia, and Patras; good Muscat dessert wines come from Crete and Samos, although the resin-flavored white Retsina and red Kokinelli are the ones that are most distinctive. They go well with Greek dishes.

Grenache [gren-ahsh]
Grape producing the best *rosé* wines, good with all sorts of foods light in taste, like fish and delicatessen, pork and veal dishes, casseroles.

Grignolino [green-yo-*lee*-no]
Light red wine, and grape, of Italy's Piedmont, good with stews and chicken, veal, and pork dishes.

Grinzing [grin-tsing]
Light and flowery white wine from the Vienna suburb of that name, good with fish and delicatessen.

Gumpoldskirchener [goom-polds-*keerk*-en-er]
The best light and flowery wine of Austria, good with fish and delicatessen.

Gyongyos-Visonta [*yong*-yohs-vee-*son*-tah]
Best sparkling white wine of Hungary, fairly sweet.

Hallgarten [*hahl*-gar-ten]
Township producing the most full-bodied of the Rheingaus, best in top years and then extremely long-lived. Vineyards producing top Hallgarteners include Schönhell and Deutelsberg; magnificent with smoked salmon, ham, or delicatessen.

Hattenheim [*haht*-en-hime]
One of the Rheingau's hillside townships, most proud of its Steinberg, the great walled vineyard near the medieval Cister-

cian monastery of Kloster Eberbach, whose *Auslesen* are among the most prized and are marketed under the vineyard name, without the town's. Others include Wisselbrunnen and Nussbrunnen, Hattenheimers of full body and fruitiness that are superb with fish, sea food, pork products, and fowl.

Haut-Brion [oh-bree-awn]
One of the greatest châteaux of Bordeaux, its red Graves is outstanding even in fair vintages, noted for its balance and bouquet, and excellent with steak, other meats, and fowl. A good dry white is also made.

Haut-Sauternes [oh-soh-tairn]
Haut means "high" in French, but it means "upper" when used with place names, and the French have used the word to imply wines with this prefix are superior. The Californians adopted the meaningless term "Haut-Sauterne (without the final "s") for sweet white wines, and use the term "Dry Sauterne" for similar, less-sweet wines. Both are quite ordinary, as are the French wines so named.

Hecto
Short for hectoliter, 100 liters, about a dozen cases.

Hermitage [air-mih-tahzh]
The Rhône district produces the longest-lived reds and dry whites of France, the reds remaining six years in cask and often living for twenty years, being excellent with hearty stews and roasts, the whites often taking five years to develop and being excellent with fish, ham, and delicatessen.

Heurige [*hoy*-rih-guh]
Austrian for new wine, particularly local whites drunk in the cafés in the Vienna suburb of Grinzing.

Hochheim [*hok*-hime]
This easternmost township of the Rheingau produces soft and fruity well-balanced wines, at their best in less-than-great years, excellent with fish and sea food, ham and pork of all kinds. Among the top Hochheimers are those from Domdechaney and Kirchenstück vineyards.

Hock

The English name for wines of the Rheingau, and, by extension, for all German white wines, taken from the first syllable of Hochheim. The English drink them as apéritifs, with fish or sea food, and smoked or spicy meats, often serving the *Auslesen* with pastries and other desserts.

Hospices de Beaune   [os-pees duh bohn]

Famous charity hospitals in Beaune to which Côte de Beaune vineyards have been donated over the years, whose wines are sold at annual auction under the name of the donor, such as "Cuvée Nicolas Rolin." Proceeds from the auction support the hospitals; while the wines are excellent, the prices are high.

Hungary

Hungary is most famous for its Tokay region, whose sweet white wines (sold in half-liter bottles holding 17 ounces) live longer than any other table wines. Red and white wines are made everywhere, but the best-known districts are Badacsony, on the shores of Lake Balaton, Somlyó to the north, Villany-Pecs to the south, and Eger, between Budapest and Tokay, in the northeast. On labels, the name of the district and the grape is used; the district names end in "i," the way of saying "of" in Hungarian, so that "Egri Bikaver" means the wine is from the Bikaver grape of Eger. They are good wines, most of them, and deserve to be better known.

Hybrid
Cross-breeding of vines produces hybrids that are more resistant to disease and more suited to local growing seasons than the pure varieties, and are developed with the aim of producing good wines in quantity. They are usually identified by the name of the hybridizer, such as Seibel, Baco, and Couderc, plus a number. They are producing some excellent wines in New York State, and elsewhere, now used mostly as parts of blends.

Inferno [een-*fair*-no]
The best of the full red wines from the Valtellina valley in Lombardy, made from the Nebbiolo grape, for serving with roasts and stews.

Iphofen [eep-*ho*-fen]
With Würzburg and Randersacker, among the biggest and best towns producing Frankenwein; Iphofeners are excellent luncheon wines to serve with fish or delicatessen.

Ischia [ees-kee-yah]
Island near Capri whose full, flowery white wines are the best of those sold as Capri; good with fish, spiced meats, and *pastas*.

Israel
Israel exports a goodly amount of wines of all types, mostly blends of fair quality from vineyards around Tel Aviv and Haifa.

Italy
The second largest wine producer (a billion gallons a year), the best of which come from the northern provinces. Barolo and Barbaresco from the Piedmont, Valtellina from Lombardy, Valpolicella and Bardolino from Veneto are the top reds, while top whites include Soave, Orvieto, and Capri. Chianti from Tuscany is often excellent. Vinification methods vary, and so does quality.

Jasnières [zha-nyair]
Light white and *rosé* wines from this small district of the Loire, near Vouvray, rarely shipped.

Jerez [hair-*eth*]
The region in southern Spain from which comes all true Sherry.

Johannisberg Riesling [yo-*han*-nis-bairg *rees*-ling]
The name, used in Switzerland and California, for Germany's Riesling grape.

Johannisberger [yo-*han*-nis-bairg-er]
Wines from the Rheingau township of Johannisberg, the most famous being Schloss Johannisberger. Full-bodied, fruity, and well-balanced, these wines are excellent with fish and delicatessen.

Josephshofer [*yo*-zefs-ho-fer]
Mosel vineyard in the town of Graach whose flowery balanced white wines are so distinguished that the town name is not used on the label. Excellent with fish, fowl, and smoked or spicy meats.

Juliénas [zhül-yay-nahs]
Beaujolais township noted for fresh, fruity reds that are Lyon favorites with fowl and meats, often drunk up within a year of the vintage.

Jura [zhü-rah]
Mountainous French region near Switzerland particularly noted for the *rosés* and white of the Arbois district, and the full, long-lived white Château-Chalon.

Jurançon [zhü-rahn-sawn]
A golden full-bodied sweet wine from this French district near the Pyrenees, drunk as an apéritif or with desserts.

Kabinettwein [kah-bee-*net*-vine]
Originally, special bottlings reserved for the owner of a German vineyard, now often indicating a superior selection of wines from a particular grower.

Kadarka [kah-*dar*-kah]
Hungarian grape producing full red wines good with roasts and stews.

Kaiserstuhl [*ky*-zur-shtool]
Volcanic slope in Baden, producing the best of the white Badischer wines, soft and flowery and light, similar to Alsatian wines from across the Rhine, good with fish and delicatessen.

Karlowitz [*kar*-lo-vitz]
Full red Yugoslavian wines from a district on the Danube.

Kellerabfüllung [*kel*-ur-*op*-fül-oong]
Literally cellar-bottled, used to identify German wines that are estate-bottled, or made at the vineyard by the owner.

Kellerabzug [*kell*-ur-op-tsoog]
Literally, "cellar-bottling," used to identify German estate-bottlings.

Kiedrich [*kee*-drik]
Hill township of the Rheingau whose fruity whites are exceptionally well-balanced in good years, especially those from the vineyards of Gräfenberg and Wasserrose, although there are several others that are also excellent with fish and smoked or spiced meats.

Knipperlé [*neep*-pair-lay]
Alsatian grape producing light white wines good with fish and delicatessen.

Königsbach [*keu*-nigs-bok]
Rheinpfalz town near Ruppertsberg, producing wines similar to those of that place, excellent with fish and smoked or spicy meats.

Kreuznach [*kroits*-nok]
Bad Kreuznach is the leading township of the Nahe district, producing full and fruity wines good with fish and delicatessen.

Kröv [kreuf]
Minor Mosel township, famous for an ordinary wine whose label shows a boy being spanked; the wine, called Nacktarsch, is a blend, the best vineyards being Niederberg and Stephansberg.

Kirsch [keersh]
Brandy made from cherries and aged in crocks, the best coming from Alsace and Bavaria. Excellent chilled, and on fruits.

Labrusca [la-*broo*-skah]
The best-known native American grape, *Vitis labrusca*; low in sugar and high in acid, wines from it have a musky tang, called foxiness, that is unpleasant when pronounced. The most common variety is Concord.

Lacrima Christi [*lah*-kree-mah *kree*-stee]
Mostly full white wines from the slopes of Vesuvius, but also a similar sparkling wine made in the Piedmont.

Lafite-Rothschild [lah-feet-roht-sheel]
Many people think Lafite is the world's greatest red wine, and it is officially rated as one of the four First Growths of the Bordeaux Médoc. Outstanding for elegance, balance, and finesse, it generally takes ten years to mature, continuing to develop for another decade, and tastes best with foods of some delicacy, like a filet of beef, a simply roasted spring chicken, terrines and *pâtés*, cheeses like Brie and Camembert.

Lambrusco [lahm-*broo*-sko]
Light red wine, usually dry and somewhat sparkling, from the Italian province of Emilia, served there mostly with fat foods like pork stews and roasts, or hearty *pastas*.

Latour [lah-toor]
Rated as one of the four First Growths of the Médoc, similar to Lafite but fuller and even longer-lived, good with roasts and meats or fowl served with sauces.

Liebfrauenstift [*leep*-frow-en-shtift]
Vineyard around the Church of Our Lady in Worms, the original *Liebfraumilch*, whose wines are fair.

Liebfraumilch [*leep*-frow-milk]
"Milk of the Blessed Virgin" is today's name for blends of white wines from Rhineland vineyards, generally blends from Sylvaner grapes from Rheinhessen vineyards, generally less than ordinary, but sometimes good.

Liter
The metric liquid measure, equaling 1.056 quarts.

Livermore
Valley in northern California's Alameda County noted for good, balanced white wines from the Sémillon, Sauvignon, and Ugni Blanc, ranging from fairly dry to sweet.

Loire [lwahr]
The river names the most extensive wine region of France. The districts along its length begin north of Nevers with Pouilly-Fumé, Sancerre, Quincey, and Reuilly, which produce flowery light whites. Then come the sweet-white-wine districts of Vouvray and Montlouis, near Tours, followed by the fruity-red-wine districts of Chinon and Bourgeuil, the whites and *rosés* of Saumur and Anjou, and ending with the flinty dry whites of Muscadet, near the river's mouth. These are, traditionally, luncheon wines, excellent with fish, casseroles and cold cuts, ham and sausage.

Lombardy
North Italian province best known for the red Valtellinas.

Luxembourg
Vineyards in the Grand Duchy lie along the upper Mosel, producing light flowery whites good with fish and delicatessen.

Madeira
The Portuguese island out in the Atlantic off the African bulge was on the Colonial trade route and its wines were early American favorites, but a century ago diseases began ravaging the vineyards, which have never recovered. These fortified wines live for decades, some century-old wines still being occasionally available. *Rainwater* was once a famous dry blend but is now a brand. Most types are named after the grape, *Sercial* being the driest. *Verdelho* is amber in color and somewhat sweet with a bitter finish; *Bual* is sweet and full; *Malvasia* is even sweeter and richer, often being called *Malmsey*. Good as apéritifs and with desserts, the sweet types are preferred because of the wines' high acidity.

Málaga [mah-lah-gah]
Sweet and rich brown dessert wine from the vineyards around Málaga, up the Mediterranean coast from Gibraltar, mostly made from Pedro Ximénez grapes and matured in the *solera* system, good with pastries and fruits. California's grape called Malaga is a table, not a wine, grape.

Malmsey
Particularly, the sweet Madeira from the Malvasia grape, and similar Malvasia wines from Spain, Italy, and the Canary Islands, good with pastries and desserts. A fifteenth-century Duke of Clarence drowned in a butt of Malmsey, source not specified.

Malvasiá di Lipari [mahl-vah-see-yah dee lee-pah-ree]
The best of the sweet, brown Italian wines made from this white grape, particularly from the islands of Salina and Stromboli. Good with pastries and fruits.

Malvoisie [mal-vwah-zee]
Sweet dark Malvasian wines of southern France, particularly Roussillon, good with desserts.

Manzanilla [mahn-thah-*neel*-lyah]
The world's driest wine, lightly fortified Fino Sherry matured in Sanlucar de Barrameda, the seacoast fishing village in the Jerez region from which Columbus sailed on his second voyage. The pale golden wine develops a special salty tang. When well-chilled it is excellent as an apéritif, or with fish, sea food, ham and spicy meats, cheeses.

Margaux [mar-go]
One of the four First Growths of the Bordeaux Médoc, so famous that the township took the name of the château, or maybe it was the other way around. Château Margaux is particularly well-balanced, softness coupled with great finesse and delicate bouquet, excellent with delicate meat or fowl dishes. Other vineyards of the township are similar, although wines labeled simply "Margaux," blends from minor vineyards, have little delicacy. See *Bordeaux*.

Marsala [mar-*sah*-lah]
Sicilian fortified wine developed for the English market by one John Woodhouse in the eighteenth century to compete with the Sherry- and Port-wine trade. Made from a variety of grapes, the amber wines range from dry to sweet, and are matured in *soleras*. Good as apéritif, and with desserts. Some are flavored with eggs, almonds, or other flavorings, which is the soda fountain approach to winemaking, not unknown elsewhere.

Marsannay-la-Côte [mar-sahn-nay-lah-koht]
Burgundy town a few miles south of Dijon, now the center for the blending of *rosé* wines made from the Pinot Noir, often good, especially with fish and delicatessen.

Maryland
Red, white, and pink wines are made from native grapes and hybrids at the experimental Boordy Vineyards of Philip M.

Wagner, *Baltimore Sun* editor; always worth trying when found on the market.

Mascara
Leading Algerian region, particularly for full-bodied red wines, occasionally available under their own names, but more often used in blends.

Mavrodaphne [mah-vro-*daf*-nee]
Sweet, red fortified Greek wine.

Maximin Grünhaus [max-íh-*meen grün*-hows]
Township on the Ruwer, a tributary of the Mosel, producing extremely light white wines, excellent in good years; fine by themselves or with fish, smoked or spicy meats.

May wine
New German wine in which *Waldmeister*, the herb woodruff, has been steeped, often served in a punch bowl with strawberries and other fruits. This is a traditional German spring drink, which can be made with any dry or flowery white wine.

Médoc [may-dok]
Bordeaux district north of the city that produces more fine red wines than any other, all the best of which are in the Upper Médoc, nearest town (the Haut Médoc). The vineyards were classified in 1855 into five numbered growths (sixty of them) and into a few Exceptional Growths, plus several hundred *Bourgeois Supérieur*, *Bourgeois*, *Artisan*, and *Paysan* Growths,

these last three mostly used for blends sold under township names. The others are marketed individually under vineyard names preceded by the word "château," to indicate that the wine was bottled at the vineyard by the grower. These château-bottlings are generally good-to-excellent red wines, superior to the regionals bearing township names, which include those marketed as Margaux, Saint Julien, Pauillac, and Saint Estèphe. They are good with all fowl and meat dishes. For vineyard listings, see *Bordeaux*.

Melnik
Good reds and whites come from this Czeckoslovakian district.

Mercurey [mair-kür-ay]
Township producing the fullest and fruitiest reds from the southern Burgundy district of Chalonnais, best when only three or four years old and excellent with meat or fowl.

Merlot [mair-lo]
Top Bordeaux red wine grape, planted in vineyards with the Cabernet Sauvignon and Cabernet Franc.

Mesnil [may-neel]
Top-rated Champagne township noted for *blanc de blancs*, excellent to serve with *foie gras*, caviar, smoked salmon, and similar sumptuous foods.

Meursault [muhr-so]
Township of Burgundy's Côte d'Or producing great whites, the best of which are estate-bottled, superb with fish, white meats, ham, and delicatessen.

Midi [mee-dee]
Large region in southern France producing wines used for blends, the *vin ordinaire* designated in French bistros by percentage of alcohol, *douze* or *onze pour-cent* (12 or 11 per cent) being considered better than lighter versions.

Millésime [meel-ay-zeem]
The vintage year. Wines that are *millésimés*, those bearing a vintage year on the bottle, are generally better than nonvintage

wines, which are blends of various vintages. The year is needed on a label in order to be sure of getting young wines before they are past their prime, as well as to avoid drinking long-to-mature wines before they have developed.

Minervois [mee-nair-vwah]
One of the better ordinary wines of the Midi.

Mise du domaine [meez dü do-main]
Literally, "bottling of the estate," a variant is *mis en bouteille*, or "put in bottle," which signifies a wine bottled at the vineyard by the grower, when accompanied by the word *domaine* or *château*; when the phrase is followed by *dans nos caves*, "in our cellars," the phrase has no meaning, for all wines are bottled in cellars.

Mittel-Haardt [*mit*-tul-*hart*]
The central district of the Rheinpfalz, whose towns (Ruppertsberg, Deidesheim, Forst, Wachenheim) produce all the best wines, which are white, fruity, full-bodied.

Moelleux [mwa-leu]
French term for soft, fruity sweet white wines like Vouvray, Saumur, Sauternes, best with desserts.

Monica [*mo*-nee-kah]
Fair sweet and fortified red wine of Sardinia.

Montagny [mawn-tan-yee]
Township producing fair fresh whites in Burgundy's Chalonnais.

Montepulciano [mon-teh-pool-*cha*-no]
Rough red of Tuscany, good with stews.

Monthélie [mawn-tay-lee]
Minor town of Burgundy's Côte d'Or, producing light, fresh reds mostly marketed without vineyard names, good with lunches of meat sandwiches, bland stews, cheese.

Montilla [mon-*teel*-lyah]
Spanish district near Cordoba producing young pale wines
rarely fortified, and lightly fortified older wines, similar to Fino
Sherries. Older wines have a full taste similar to Amontillado
sherries, which were named after them. Good as apéritif, with
fish and delicatessen, when chilled.

Montlouis [mawn-lwee]
Township near Vouvray, producing sweet, flowery whites once
marketed as Vouvray, good with fish and delicatessen.

Montrachet [mawn-rah-shay]
The world's greatest dry white wine comes from Le Montrachet
vineyard, and similar but less full whites come from adjoining
vineyards permitted by law to add the famous name to their
own. The vineyard extends across the town boundary of Puligny
and into Chassagne, both of which have also added "Montrachet" to their names, so that all the wines of the towns can
be marketed bearing the magic word. Consequently, the actual
vineyard name must appear on the label to insure getting the
great wine, which is magnificent with fish and sea food, terrines
and galantines, ham and delicatessen. See *Burgundy*.

Morey-St.-Denis [mo-ray-san-duh-nee]
One of the great wine towns of Burgundy's Côte de Nuits, just
south of Gevrey-Chambertin, the red wines being only slightly
lighter and less full than the Chambertins. Top vineyards are
Bonnes-Mares, Clos de la Roche, Clos Saint-Denis, and Clos
de Tart, but there are a dozen other First Growths, notably
Clos des Lambrays. These are not as well known as many other
Burgundies, and are often more reasonable in price. They take
five or six years to mature, taste best with poultry and wildfowl,
beef and game, terrines and *pâtés*, stews and roasts.

Morgon [mor-gawn]
Beaujolais township, producing fullest of these red wines, good
with stews and roasts.

Moscato [mo-*skah*-to]
Italian wines from the Muscat grape, including the almost-sweet, sparkling Asti Spumante from the Piedmont, and especially the sweet wines from Apulia, Calabria, Sicily, and Sardinia, to serve with pastries, fruit, other desserts.

Mosel [*mo*-zul]
German name for the wine district on the banks of that river, which empties into the Rhine but rises in the French Vosges, so the German wines have become known as Moselles.

Moselblümchen [*mo*-zul-blüm-ken]
"Mosel blossoms" are blends from minor vineyards along the German river, about on a par with the Liebfraumilch of the Rheinhessen, but lighter, flowerier, and good for lunch with fish or cold cuts.

Moselle [mo-*zell*]
The lightest of the German wines, the best of which come from the Mittel-Mosel, some thirty miles of the world's steepest vineyards between Traben-Trarbach and Trittenheim, endlessly varying although all are made from the Riesling. Like them are the wines from vineyards along the tributaries of the Saar and the Ruwer, which join the Mosel near Trier. The wines are delicious by themselves, but are often served with delicate luncheon dishes like grilled fish, veal or ham with light sauces, delicatessen, and cheese dishes. They are best when between two and five years old, although the *Auslesen* often last for ten years when the vintage is good. See *Germany*.

Moulin-à-Vent [moo-la-nah-von]
The best-known and fullest of the Beaujolais township wines, excellent with roasts or stews of meat or fowl.

Moulis [moo-lee]
Township near Margaux in the Bordeaux Haut Médoc, producing full reds good with meat or fowl. See *Bordeaux*.

Mountain

The English called Málaga reds this a couple of centuries ago, and now the word is used in California, particularly the Napa and Sonoma valleys, for good blends of inexpensive reds and whites.

Mousseux [moo-seu]

The French use the term *vin mousseux*, "foaming wine," for any sparkling wine not entitled to be called Champagne, which includes all wines produced outside the district, such as Vouvray Mousseux.

Mouton-Rothschild [moo-tawn-roht-sheel]

One of the five greatest red wines of the Bordeaux Médoc, often taking six years to mature, even longer in great years, but then full and intense, excellent with roasts of meat and game, poultry and wildfowl, or these served with rich sauces or in terrines.

Muscadet [mü-skah-day]

Light, dry wines best when only two or three years old, once used to stretch the short supply of Chablis, now marketed under its own district name, and good with fish, spicy dishes, delicatessen.

Muscadine

Native American grape species once widely grown in the South, most popular being the musky white Scuppernong.

Muscatel

In Europe, various muscat grapes are used to produce a variety of fair wines, particularly the sweet Muscat de Frontignan of southern France. California Muscatel is generally made from a table grape, the Alexandria, which makes poor wine.

Musigny [mü-zeen-yee]
One of the greatest red Burgundies, the vineyard being in the
town of Chambolle in the Côte de Nuits. Soft and full, it
takes some five years to mature in good years, lives for a decade
longer and more. Serve with meat and game, poultry and wildfowl.

Nackenheim
The top wine town of the Rheinhessen; the best are full, soft
Rieslings from such vineyards as Rothenberg and Engelsberg,
good with fish, veal and pork with light sauces, ham and delicatessen.

Nahe [*nah*-uh]
River that empties into the Rhine near Bingen, whose vineyards are on the steep valley slopes and produce soft, full wines
from the towns of Kreuznach, Schloss Bockelheim, Norheim,
Niederhausen, Münster, Roxheim. Good with fish and delicatessen.

Napa
Valley north of San Francisco producing some of the best Cali-
fornia wines, particularly those marketed under grape names.
Leading producers include Inglenook, Beaulieu Vineyards,
Louis Martini, Krug.

Naturwein [nah-*toor*-vine]
In Germany the phrase for wine made from grape juice that
has not been sugared, something often necessary for thin wines
from northern vineyards. Estate-bottled German wines are
never sugared, and the word appears on the label. Regionals
are often good, even though sugared; such wines do not taste
sweet, for the sugar is converted to alcohol.

Nebbiolo [nehb-*byo*-lo]
The greatest Italian red wine grape, planted mostly in the Piedmont and Lombardy, from which are made Barolo, Barbaresco,
Gattinara, and the Valtellina wines of Inferno, Sassella, Valgella, and Grumello. Full, balanced wines that require at least

three years to mature, they are excellent with full-flavored meat or game, poultry or wildfowl, particularly those served with brown sauces.

New York
Noted for its white wines, still and sparkling, from native grapes and hybrids, particularly from the Finger Lakes region, although there are some vineyards on the Hudson and in Chautauqua County. Good with fish, delicatessen, luncheon dishes.

Niagara
Peninsula between Lake Erie and Lake Ontario, where most of Canada's wines are produced, the best being white and similar to those of New York State.

Niederhausen [*nee*-der-how-zen]
One of the top Nahe townships, among the best vineyards being Hermannsberg and Hermannshöhle.

Niedermennig [nee-der-*men*-ick]
Top Saar township; vineyards include Sonnenberg, Euchariusberg. Its light wines are best with lunch.

Nierstein [*neer*-shtine]
Top wine town of the Rheinhessen, Rieslings noted for their full ripeness; top vineyards include Rehbach and Hipping, superb with fish, particularly those served with sauces, with veal, and delicatessen.

Norheim [*nor*-hime]
Top district of the Nahe; vineyards include Kafels, Kirscheck.

North Coast Counties
Countryside near San Francisco that produces all the top wines of California, marketed under grape names. These "varietals" come from vineyards in Napa, Sonoma, Contre Costa, Alameda, Santa Clara, and Santa Cruz, and parts of Mendocino and Solano.

Nuits-St.-Georges [nwee-san-zhorzh]
Southernmost and largest town of Burgundy's Côte de Nuits,

producing full, big-bodied wines that often take five years to mature, excellent with beef and other meats, game and fowl. See *Burgundy*.

Oberemmel   [o-ber-*em*-ul]
Good township of the Saar, producing light, flowery wines in great years, Hütte and Rosenberg being fine vineyards. Oberemmelers are so light that they are best by themselves, or with grilled fish or a soufflé.

Ockfen
Saar township on a par with Oberemmel, although Ockfeners excel in very great years, particularly Bockstein and Herrenberg.

Œil de perdrix   [euy duh pare-dree]
White wines made from black grapes, particularly Champagnes, develop a gray-pink cast, the color of a "partridge's eye," which is a sign of maturity.

Ohio
White wines made from the Catawba and Delaware are made around Sandusky and on Lake Erie islands, as are some good sparkling wines.

Oloroso   [oh-lo-*ro*-so]
Full dark Sherries that need at least ten years to mature, and usually more, to which old and expensive sweetening wines are added for export; excellent with pastries and fruits, particularly melons, or in the afternoon with cakes or puddings.

Oppenheim
Major town of the Rheinhessen, producing soft and fruity wines from vineyards like Sackträger and Kreuz, excellent with fish and sea food served with sauces.

Originalabfüllung   [oh-*rig*-ih-nal-*ap*-fül-loong]
Original bottling, one of the German phrases on a label that signifies an estate-bottling, a wine bottled by the grower.

Orvieto   [or-*vyeh*-to]
The white peer of Chianti, sold as *secco* or *abboccato*, dry or slightly sweet, and marketed in the straw-covered *fiaschi* used for Chianti; dries often good with *pastas*, fish, and delicatessen.

Östrich   [*eust*-rish]
Good Rheingau town producing soft, full wines, like lesser Hallgarteners, best vineyards being Lenchen and Doosberg.

Ouillage   [wee-yahzh]
What's lost when a cask or bottle leaks, or the loss by evaporation. An ullaged bottle is apt to hold spoiled wine.

Palatinate
The Counts Palatine came from the Rheinpfalz, and the district is often called the Palatinate, extending from the French border north beyond Bad Durkheim. The best wines come from the Mittel-Haardt, the name for the hills that range the district's length, and on whose slopes are the vineyards of Ruppertsberg, Deidesheim, Forst, and Wachenheim.

Passito   [pahs-*see*-to]
Sweet wines made from raisinized grapes in Italy, mostly drunk between meals as a tonic or cordial.

Pasteurization
Pasteur was the first to make major discoveries about fermentation, developing the way of heating wines to destroy bacteria, useful for wines that have begun to acetify or otherwise go bad. The wine is stabilized at a low level, tasting bland and flat. No

fine wines are ever pasteurized; if a fine wine is pasteurized it is sold as a regional, not under a famous vineyard name.

Patras [pa-*trahs*]
Good white Greek wine.

Patrimonio [pa-tree-*mo*-nyo]
Corsican wines, best of which is *rosé*, good with hearty fish dishes or meat stews.

Pauillac [po-ee-yak]
Township boasting three of the four top vineyards of Bordeaux's Haut Médoc, and fifteen other Classified Growths, the wines generally being balanced and soft, with full bouquets. It is the largest township, but regionals bearing the town name are rarely seen. Good wines to serve with meat and fowl simply cooked or served with light sauces, with terrines or *pâtés*.

Pedro Ximénez [*peh*-dro he-*may*-neth]
Grape originally brought from Germany, used to make wines for sweetening Oloroso Sherries, and to make Málagas and Montillas. When old, the wine is very dark, sweet, and rich.

Pelure d'oignon [puh-lür dawn-yawn]
"Onion skin" is the color some red wines turn to as they get old; the deep brown tinge around the rim of the glass is a sign of maturity.

Pernand-Vergelesses [pair-nahn-vair-zhuh-les]
Good wine village of Burgundy's Côte de Beaune, up the slope behind Aloxe-Corton, with vineyards adjoining Corton, some good ones not well known and usually reasonable in price. See *Burgundy*.

Pétillant [pay-tee-yahn]
French word for wines with a light sparkle or crackle, fresh and fizzy on the tongue. Light wines often develop this characteristic in the spring, such as Vouvray, Alsatians, and Swiss wines, where the characteristic is called "the star."

Pétrus [pay-trüs]
Best vineyard of Pomerol, whose wines are full, stout, and rich, often taking ten years to round out, excellent with pork, veal, and beef roasts, or any meat or fowl with dark sauces, and cheese.

Pfalz [fahltz]
The Rheinpfalz, or Palatinate, famous for full Rieslings. See *Germany*.

Piedmont
Italy's northern province and best wine region, noted for reds from the Nebbiolo grape, and other good ones from the Freisa, Barbera, and Grignolino. See *Italy*.

Pinard [pee-nar]
French slang for cheap red wine.

Pinot [pee-no]
Name for the great Burgundy grapes—the red Pinot Noir, the white Pinot Chardonnay, responsible for all the great wines except the Meursaults, which are made from Pinot Blanc. The Pinot Gris is grown in Alsace. The Pineau de la Loire is the Chenin Blanc, not a Pinot, but its wines are called White Pinot in California. The true Pinots produce good wines nearly everywhere, but all their great wines come from Burgundy.

Pipe
The name for Port and Madeira casks, which have small ends and usually hold 126 gallons.

Piqué [pee-kay]
A *piqué* wine is one that has been "pricked," and is turning to vinegar, or already turned.

Piquette [pee-ket]
A cheap sort of wine made by mixing sugar and water with the caked pulp left after the pressing.

Pomerol [pom-rohl]
One of the five great Bordeaux wine districts, noted for full,

soft, long-lived wines excellent with hearty meats and fowl, often taking ten years to mature. See *Bordeaux*.

Port

The great wine of Portugal, from vineyards on the Upper Douro river, where brandy is added during the pressing to preserve the natural grape sugar in the wine. *Ruby Port* is a blend of young wines, while paler blends of older wines are termed *Tawny Port*. *Vintage Port* is aged in casks for two years, then bottled in the country where it is to be drunk, twenty years later; most of this goes to England. *Crusted Port* is young Port bottled promptly and allowed to mature in the bottle, where it forms a crust. *White Ports* are made from white grapes, occasionally blended with red Ports to make young Tawnies. Similar wines made elsewhere rarely reach the level of well-shipped Port, as the fine wines are called. True Port is an excellent conclusion to a meal, the bottle being passed clockwise around the table, fruit, nuts, and cheese being served with it, traditionally. Perfect with melons and not-too-sweet desserts.

Portugal

The fourth largest wine producer, after France, Italy, and Spain. Most of the wines are young, sharp *vinho verde*—"green wine" that is actually red, white, or pink—and rough reds, the best from Collares. Medium sweet whites are Setubal and Bucellas. These are rarely shipped.

Pot [po]

A half-liter bottle used in the Beaujolais.

Pouilly-Fuissé [pwee-yee-fwee-say]

One of the great dry white Burgundies, produced in the district of Mâconnais, near Beaujolais. Full-bodied and well-balanced, the wines take three years to develop, often live for a decade. These are the classic wines the French serve with *charcuterie*, the viands of the pork butcher that include terrines and *pâtés*, sausages and delicatessen.

Pouilly-Fumé [pwee-yee-fü-may]

The best wine from the district called Pouilly-sur-Loire, sometimes called Blanc-Fumé, made from the Bordeaux grape, Sauvignon Blanc. It is fresh and flowery with a crispness that suits it for drinking with ham and spicy dishes, fish and delicatessen. Best when only two or three years old, it is past its prime at five. Lesser wines marketed under the district name are made from the Chasselas grape.

Pourriture noble   [poor-rih-tür nohbl]
The "noble rot" is a mold that attacks late-picked grapes, making Sauternes and the German *Auslesen* what they are: rich, sweet, and fruity.

Puligny-Montrachet   [poo-leen-yee-mawn-rah-shay]
Town producing great dry white Burgundies, including the greatest, Le Montrachet. See *Burgundy*. Magnificent with fish, white meats, delicatessen.

Quart de Chaume   [car duh shohm]
The best of the minor wines of France, an astonishing balance of lightness and bouquet coupled with fresh fruitiness and high alcohol, often 14 per cent. The "Quarter of Chaume" is in the Anjou sub-district of Coteaux du Layon. The white wine develops in two years, is past its prime at seven or eight, and is excellent with foods that have a sweet savor (like lobster or crabmeat) and with smoky, spicy, or fat delicatessen.

Quetsch   [kwetch]
A distillate from purple plums, white because it is stored in crocks after first aging in wood for a short time. Generally served with fruits or after meals, often chilled.

Quincy [can-see]
Flowery dry white of the Upper Loire township, good when two years old. Made from the Sauvignon Blanc grape of Bordeaux, it is good with fish and delicatessen.

Racking
Drawing the wine off the sediment, the lees, left in a cask after the wine has been cleared.

Rainwater
A dry, soft Madeira good as an apéritif.

Rancio [ran-see-oh]
The Sherry-like taste acquired by some French sweet wines, like those of Banyuls, when they have matured for several years. The wines are drunk as apéritifs.

Rauenthal [*row*-en-tahl]
Hill town of Germany's Rheingau, celebrated in Germany as producing the finest wines, having a balance of ripeness and fruitiness, particularly from such vineyards as Baiken and Gehrn. ·Superb with fish served with a sauce, or similar fowl, pork, or veal dishes, and with sea food.

Rheingau [*rine*-gow]
The most important of the Rhineland districts, producing a galaxy of full-bodied, fruity, balanced wines from the Riesling grape from vineyards along a twenty-mile stretch on the north bank of the Rhine, between Hochheim and Rudesheim. Vineyard names on the label are necessary for superior wines; the best are estate-bottled. Served by themselves or with fish, sea food, fowl, and white meats simply cooked or served with light or white sauces, and with delicatessen. See *Germany*.

Rheinhessen [rine-*hess*-en]
Major Rhineland district producing some excellent soft Rieslings and many flowery Sylvaners, good with fish, sea food, and delicatessen. Most important towns are Nackenheim, Nierstein, and Oppenheim. See *Germany*.

Rheinpfalz [*rine*-fahltz]
Major Rhineland district producing full-bodied, fruity Rieslings
and fresh Sylvaners, good with fish and sea food, white meats
with light sauces, ham and delicatessen. Best townships are
Forst, Deidesheim, Rupertsberg, and Wachenheim. See *Germany*.

Rhine wine
General term for wines from districts along the Rhine and its
tributaries, including Alsace and the German districts incor-
porating the river's name in their own, and including for sim-
plicity the wines of the Mosel because that river flows into the
Rhine. All the best wines are white, although some ordinary
reds are made. Top wines come from the Riesling grape, but
excellent Sylvaners and Traminers are made. They are generally best by themselves, or with fish and sea food, ham and
delicatessen, and the top wines are excellent ..ith white meats
served with light sauces. They are ready to drink after two
years, often past their prime after five, although *Auslesen* may
live for ten years and more. See *Germany*.

Rhône
Wine districts of this region are along the river, beginning with
Côte Rôtie, Condrieu, and Château Grillet, south of Lyons,
including Hermitage near Valence, and Châteauneuf-du-Pape
and Tavel, near Avignon. They are south of Burgundy, and are
often grouped with Burgundies, which they somewhat resemble.
They are full-bodied, long-lived wines, the whites excellent with
fish and sea food, white and smoked meats, the reds excellent
with roasts and stews and meats served with hearty sauces. The
whites are generally ready to drink after two years, and past
their prime at five, although white Hermitage takes an extra
year or so to develop and lives for a decade. The reds often
take five years to mature, often live for twenty. The *rosé* wines
of Tavel are ready two years after the vintage, past their peak
at five years, and are served like whites.

Richebourg [reesh-boorg]
One of the greatest red Burgundies of the Côte de Nuits, very
full-bodied, often taking five years to mature, excellent with
roasts and hearty meat or fowl dishes.

Riesling [*rees*-ling]
The outstanding German wine grape from which come all the
great German wines. It produces excellent to good wines elsewhere, and is known as Johannisberg Riesling in California.

Rioja [ree-*o*-hah]
Region in northern Spain producing the country's best reds and
whites, which are usually blends from various vintages and
grapes. The reds often need five years to develop, the soft and
flowery, sometimes sweet, whites are ready after three years.
Good to serve with Spanish dishes, casseroles, and hearty rice
or meat dishes.

Romanée [ro-mah-nay]
Four of Burgundy's greatest Côte de Nuits vineyards have
Romanée in their names, the most delicate in body and richest
in bouquet being Romanée-Conti (4 acres), followed by the
slightly fuller La Romanée (2 acres) and Romanée-La Tâche
(6½ acres), this last marketed simply as La Tâche. Romanée-
St. Vivant has 24 acres and is the fullest of the wines of Vosne-
Romanée, much like Richebourg, the other great vineyard of
the township. These reds often need ten years to mature, can

live for decades, and are an unbelievable combination of delicacy and intensity, most often served with prime beef or veal, with wildfowl or poultry, simply roasted or grilled, or served with delicate sauces.

Rosé [ro-zay]
The French name for pink wines, made by drawing off the fermenting juice from the pulpy mass of the black grapes, so that color is not picked up from the skins. The best *rosés* are considered to be those of Tavel, made from the Grenache grape, which also produces well in California. Those from Arbois and the Touraine are also well thought of. All three are well-blended wines, ready to drink after two years, past their prime after five. Every wine district produces pink wines, the Italians calling theirs *rosatos*. The *rosés* are not often drunk when good whites or reds are available, but they are popular with hostesses because they can be served with dishes that call for white wines or light reds, such as fish, light stews, casseroles, and delicatessen. The wines taste good with almost anything, and should be chilled.

Roussillon [roo-see-yawn]
District of southern France producing hearty reds and heady *rosés*, but best known for such sweet wines as Banyuls.

Rudesheim [*roo*-des-hime]
Township producing the fullest whites of the Rheingau, best in vintages rated fair or good, outstanding wines coming from a single *Berg*, or hill. Good with fish and sea food, lightly sauced meats, and delicatessen.

Rufina [roo-*fee*-nah]
Township near the Chianti district, whose fruity red wines are often shipped as Chianti, good with meat and stews.

Rully [rü-yee]
Township of the Chalonnais in southern Burgundy, producing an ordinary red wine, often made sparkling.

Ruppertsberg [*roo*-pehrts-bairg]
Top town of the Rheinpfalz, the fine vineyards include Gaisböhl and Spiess, whose wines are excellent with fish and sea food, ham and delicatessen.

Ruwer [*roo*-vair]
Mosel tributary producing exceptionally light and dry but very flowery wines in such townships as Eitelsbach, Maximin Grünhaus, and Kasel. Good only in fine vintages, they taste best by themselves, but are served with fish, ham, and delicatessen.

Saar [zahr]
Mosel tributary noted for light, intense Rieslings, with a *stahlig*, or steely quality, outstanding only in good and great years, the top township being Wiltingen, followed by Oberemmel, Ayl, and Ockfen. These wines are ready within two years of the vintage, past their prime at five years. Best by themselves, they also taste good with smoked salmon, soufflés made of fish or light cheeses, and light delicatessen.

Sack
An ancient English name for heavy southern wines, Canary, Madeira, and particularly Sherry. Probably from the Spanish *saco*, meaning to export.

St. Amour [san-ta-moor]
Beaujolais township producing very light reds, excellent with chicken or veal stews.

St. Émilion [san-tay-mee-yawn]
One of the five top Bordeaux districts, producing full, fruity reds dubbed the Burgundies of Bordeaux, made mostly from Cabernet Franc. They take at least five years to develop. Top vineyards are Ausone and Cheval Blanc, but there are several others with high official ratings. Not as distinctive as the Médoc reds, they are good with hearty meats, game, and fowl, particularly those served with brown sauces.

St. Estèphe [san-teh-stef]
One of the top townships of Bordeaux's Haut Médoc, whose

Classified Growths include Cos d'Estournel, Montrose, and Calon-Ségur, full-bodied wines even in fair years, taking five years to mature, and excellent with roasts and grillades of meat or fowl. The local cooperative produces an excellent regional.

St. Julien [san zhül-yan]
A top town of the Bordeaux Haut Médoc, which boasts of many Classified Growths, and whose regionals are popular. The wines are fairly full-bodied, with a big bouquet, take five years to mature, and are good with roasts and grillades of meat or fowl. See *Bordeaux*.

St. Nicholas [san nee-co-lah]
Small Loire district whose complete name is St. Nicholas-de-Bourgeuil, red wine fuller and fruitier than Bourgeuil, excellent with roasts and stews when less than five years old.

St. Péray [san pay-ray]
Minor township of the Rhône, producing ordinary whites.

Sancerre [san-sair]
Small district across the Loire from Pouilly-sur-Loire, producing fragrant white wines from the Sauvignon Blanc, best township being Chavignol. Serve with fish, delicatessen.

Santa Maddalena [*sahn*-tah mad-dah-*lay*-nah]
Full, distinctive red wine from the Venetian countryside, good with roasts and stews.

Santenay [sahn-tuh-nay]
The southernmost town of the Côte d'Or, producing some good light red wines more like Chalonnais wines than those of the Golden Slope, good with meats.

Sardinia
The island produces a variety of full wines, particularly Vernaccia, which is like a dry Fino Sherry; a sweet version is made. Sweet reds like Monica and Giro are popular with desserts, as are the golden Moscatos and Malvasias. The red Oliena is served with meats, the amber Vermentino with fish and *pastas*.

Sassella [sas-*sel*-la]
One of the best reds from the Valtellina valley of Lombardy, excellent with meats.

Saumur [so-mür]
Famous town in the Anjou, noted for its sweet or sparkling white wines, often drunk with fish and sea food served with a sauce.

Sauternes [so-tairn]
The sweet-white-wine district of Bordeaux, with which Barsac is generally coupled, producing rich, full wines made from grapes of the Sémillon and Cabernet Sauvignon that have shriveled because of a mold whose action is called the *pourriture noble,* or "noble rot." It is the same as the *Edelfaule* of Germany, which is responsible for *Auslesen* wines of high quality. The greatest of the pale golden Sauternes is Château d'Yquem, although many others were classified in 1855. See *Bordeaux.* The name has been taken over in California, the "s" being dropped, where it is attached to dry and sweet white wines, rarely better than fair. The French Sauternes are excellent with dishes that have a sweet savor, like creamed lobster or baked ham with fruit, but are best with custardy desserts and flaky pastries or moist cakes.

Sauvignon Blanc [so-veen-yawn blahn]
Fine white wine grape producing soft and flowery wines, particularly in the Bordeaux districts of Graves and Sauternes, where it is planted with Sémillon; also used on the Upper Loire. Good wines are made from it in California's Livermore Valley.

Savigny-les-Beaune [sa-veen-yee-lay-bohn]
Large township adjoining Beaune that produces some good reds
and whites, generally sold under the township name; luncheon
wines to be served with light dishes.

Savoie [sa-vwah]
The Savoy district in the French Alps is noted for the dry
white **Seyssel**, and for good, fresh sparkling wines.

Scharzberg [shartz-*bairg*]
Famous vineyard of Wiltingen, the best Saar township, that
is marketed under its own name, not the town's. The Scharzhofberg is a similar vineyard. They are light and flowery in good
years, and have great finesse and a steely quality in great ones,
best when served by themselves or with light foods like fish or
delicatessen.

Schaumwein [*showm*-vine]
German name for sparkling wine, usually poor.

Schillerwein [*shill*-er-vine]
Name for South German wines with a slight shimmer or sparkle, particularly the ordinary pink wines of Württemberg.

Schloss Böckelheim [shloss *buk*-el-hime]
One of the best townships of the Nahe, producing soft wines
excellent with fish and sea food.

Schloss Johannisberger [shloss yo-*hahn*-nis-bairg-er]
Perhaps the most famous vineyard of the Rheingau, and the
best wine from the town of Johannisberg, but with many peers
in Rüdesheim, Winkel, Hattenheim, Erbach, and Rauenthal,
which may be more full-bodied and fruity, but rarely equal the
Johannisbergers in balance and finesse. Excellent with fish, and
dishes served with white sauces.

Schloss Vollrads [shloss *fohl*-rahts]
One of the greatest Rheingau vineyards, its wines are noted
for great fruitiness and distinction. In the town of Winkel, and
not far from Schloss Johannisberg, its neighbors have similar

qualities. See *Germany*. Excellent with fish and white meats served with sauces.

Sec
The French for dry, applied particularly to wines that are not sweet to the taste, although they may be fruity or flowery. In Champagnes, *sec* means a lightly sweet wine, while *Extra-sec* means a drier, flowery wine and one that is better with food than the extremely dry *Brut*.

Sediment
Wines are living things, and cast a deposit after years in bottle. This does not hurt the wine, and is a sign that the wine has matured, but the sediment does not taste good, and care needs be taken to see that the sediment does not come out with the wine when it is poured, or that the bottle is not shaken before serving. Today, wine buyers are wary of sediment, so that wines are overfiltered before being bottled, which tends to shorten their life and blunt their taste.

Seewein   [*zay*-vine]
Pleasant wines, rarely shipped, from the vineyards around Lake Constance, which is called the Bodensee in German.

Sekt
German term for bottle-fermented sparkling wines.

Sémillon   [seh-mee-yawn]
With the Sauvignon, the outstanding white grape of Bordeaux, producing good dry, flowery wines in California.

Sercial   [*sair*-syahl]
Grape, and dry white wine, of Madeira.

Setubal   [set-oo-*bahl*]
Portugese township producing good, sweet Muscatel.

Seyssel   [say-sell]
Excellent sharp, dry white wine from the Savoie, good to serve with fish, cheese dishes, delicatessen.

Sherry

The great wine of Spain, made primarily from the Palomino grape on chalky soil in the region near the southern city of Jerez, and matured in the *solera* system. If a yeast called the *flor*, or flower, forms on the surface during fermentation, Sherries of the *Fino* type are made, which take seven to ten years to mature; certain coarse Finos take longer, and these develop a nutty taste, and are called *Amontillados*. These dry Sherries are excellent apéritifs, and good wines to serve with fish, sea food, spicy dishes like casseroles or Oriental foods, and soups. If the *flor* does not develop on the wines, the Sherry becomes an *Oloroso*, or fragrant sherry; these are sweetened for export, with aged sweetening wines, to become the *Cream, Brown* or *East India Sherries* so famous in England. Olorosos sent to the United States are excellent with desserts, particularly melons, or in place of dessert. Customarily, a wine dinner begins with a well-chilled dry Sherry, either a Fino or an Amontillado. A special kind of Fino, extremely dry and with a salty tang, is produced in Sanlucar, a seacoast town in the district; this *Manzanilla* is popular in Spain for drinking as an apéritif, with cheese, ham, almonds, or other hors d'oeuvre.

Sicily

The island is famous for Marsala, but good, sweet Moscato is made, and full reds at Faro and Etna, the last also producing a dry white. Excellent with local dishes, but the table wines are rarely exported.

Soave   [so-*ah*-veh]

The best white wine of Italy, from near Verona, dry but flowery, best when drunk young, past prime after five years, excellent with *pastas*, fish, delicatessen.

Somlyó   [*shom*-loy]

Hungarian district producing flowery, dry white wines, good with fish and delicatessen.

South Africa

Large wine-producing area similar to California, whose best

wines come from Constantia, Stellenbosch, and the Paarl Valley; much drunk in England, rare elsewhere.

South America
Chile is the most important wine exporter in South America, producing excellent whites from the Riesling and other grapes, good reds from French and Italian grapes. The wines are low in price and good buys when not too old, the whites for serving with fish, *pastas*, and delicatessen, the reds with meats.

Spain
Third largest in production, after France and Italy, the best table wines are from the Rioja, although red Valdepeñas can be good. The great Spanish wine is Sherry, a fortified wine poorly copied in other countries; others include the sweet Málaga and Tarragona. Montilla is lightly fortified, and a good apéritif.

Spätlese [*shpait*-lay-zuh]
Name for a German wine made from late-picked grapes that contain less juice but more sugar, and produce a fuller, fruitier, sweeter wine. Every vineyard owner tries to make at least a few casks because the richer wines command higher prices than does the *Naturwein*, made from grapes of normal ripeness. *Spätlese* wines are good with rich or fat foods—buttery fish or lobster, a smoky ham or pork roast. They are often served with dishes with a sweet savor or a creamy sauce.

Spumante [spoo-*mon*-tee]
The Italian word for sparkling wines, generally too sweet and often poor.

Steinberger [*shtine*-bair-ger]
Great vineyard of the Rheingau, a full wine ranking with the best, owned by the German government. Excellent with foods served with a white sauce, fish, and delicatessen.

Switzerland
Dry, flowery light white wines come from Neuchâtel, La Côte and Lavaux, on the north shores of Lake Geneva, and the

Valais. Every canton produces wine, including reds called Dôle de Sion, and most of them are well made, to be drunk before they are three years old. The Fendant grape, actually the French Chasselas, produces most of the wines, although the Riesling, here called the Johannisberg, is also grown. The wines are excellent with cheeses and cheese dishes, with fish and delicatessen.

Sylvaner [sil-*vah*-ner]
Good German grape responsible for many wines of Hesse and the Palatinate, and also Alsatians, fairly fresh and fruity, particularly good with fish and delicatessen. This grape is called the Riesling in California, where it makes fair wines.

Tâche [tosh]
La Tâche is a great Burgundy vineyard in the township of Vosne-Romanée, but the town name is not used on the label. Very full and well-balanced, it takes five years to mature, and is excellent with meat and game, poultry and wildfowl.

Tannin
A sharp-tasting acid imparted to wines from the seeds and stems, useful in helping the wine to age properly and in keeping it clear, but lending an unpleasant sharpness when too pronounced.

Tarragona [tar-rah-*go*-nah]
Dark red, sweet Spanish wine made to resemble Port, but rarely good.

Tavel [tah-vel]
Rhône district celebrated for its *rosé* wines, made from the Grenache grape. Best when young, blends from various vineyards taste good with most foods, particularly fish and mild stews, or meats with light sauces. Should be chilled.

Tokay [*to*-kye]
Very sweet, pungent wine from the famous Hungarian region. Made from Furmint grapes, the wine lives for decades and has an astonishing tonic quality. The best is *Tokay Aszu*, made by adding baskets, called *puttonyos*, of overripe grapes to normally ripened ones; the wine is identified by the number of *puttonyos* added. *Tokay Szamorodni* is made without adding overripe grapes. Years ago, *Tokay Eszencia*, made from the oozings from the *puttonyos*, was produced, but this is rarely found today. The wines live for decades. They are so precious, they are shipped in small half-liter bottles. They are drunk at the end of the meal, by themselves, and occasionally with cakes and other desserts.

Touraine [too-ren]
Wine region of the Loire noted for Vouvrays and Chinons.

Traben-Trarbach [*trah*-ben-*trar*-bok]
Twin villages on each side of the Mosel, marking the downstream limit of the fine-wine section. Its own light, fresh wines come from such vineyards as Schlossberg and Huhnersberg, particularly flowery in good years, tasting best with fish and delicatessen.

Traminer [trah-*mee*-ner]
Distinguished grape of Alsace and the adjoining Rheinpfalz, ranking just below the noble Riesling and Chardonnay among white-wine grapes. Wines are full and flowery, while a strain called Gewürztraminer has a spicy freshness that warrants its name. These are excellent wines with a Strasbourg *choucroute garni*, or a lunch of hot potato salad and thinly sliced delicatessen, or meats served with sharp sauces, or the local *truite au bleu*.

Trebbiano [treb-*byah*-no]
Italian name for the Ugni Blanc, used to make Chianti.

Trockenbeerenauslese [*truk*-en-bair-en-*ows*-lay-zuh]
"Dried berry selection" is the translation for the highest class of German wines, made from a selection of dried berries from selected bunches attacked by the *Edelfaule*. Now rare, very expensive, very sweet, drunk on occasions by itself.

Ugni Blanc [oo-nyee blahn]
White wine grape used in Cognac vineyards, and also in Chianti vineyards.

Ürzig [*ür*-tsik]
Fine wine town of the Mittel-Mosel noted for wines with a spicy sharpness that are often slightly sparkling, or *spritzig*. Among the top vineyards are Würzgarten and Schwarzlay. The wines are thin and acid in poor years, but their sprightly taste in fine years makes them delightful to drink with dishes that employ ham or bacon in the preparation, or with fish and sea food.

Valdepeñas [val-deh-*pain*-yas]
Spanish region producing full, inexpensive wines, occasional reds being good with sauced meats and stews.

Valpolicella [val-poh-lee-*chel*-lah]
Good red table wine from Venetia, full of tannin when young, but after four years developing smoothness and a good bouquet, generally served with roasts and stews.

Valtellin
A pale, golden dessert wine from Hungary.

Valtellina [val-tel-*lee*-nah]
Valley in Lombardy producing, from the Nebbiolo grape, full, balanced red wines from near Sondrio, called Sassella, Inferno, Grumello, and Valgella. The wines take perhaps four years to mature, and are then ready to serve with meat and fowl.

Varietal
Wine marketed under the grape name, a system used for California's best wines.

Verdiso [vair-*dee*-zo]
Fresh, dry white wine from near Venice, excellent with fish, sea food, *pastas*.

Vermouth
Hard, dry wines infused with an assortment of herbs, primarily wormwood blossoms, then aged in casks. Italian Vermouths come from Turin, and the dark, sweet ones are best known, although dry Vermouths and bitter Vermouths are also made. French Vermouths are generally dry; the center of production is Marseilles, but particularly dry, light Vermouths come from Chambéry, in the Savoy. Good chilled, as an apéritif. Often mixed with gin.

Vernaccia [vair-*noch*-cha]
Heady dry white, particularly those from Sardinia, the dry ones being like a very dry Fino Sherry.

Verzenay [vair-zuh-nay]
Township in the Champagne region, producing *blanc de noirs*, whose vineyards have a 100 per cent rating. See *Champagne*.

Vesuvio [veh-zoo-vee-o]
Good dry white wine from the slopes of Vesuvius, good with *pastas*, fish, and delicatessen.

Vin de Paille [van duh py]
Grapes are laid on straw mats to dry, and the wines are sweet and golden when made. Good ones come from the Jura, usually served with desserts, or after.

Vin du pays [van dü pay-ee]
Country wines, or local wines, generally good but too light or scarce to be shipped, and generally drunk out of curiosity, if for no other reason, by knowing travelers.

Vin Gris [van gree]
Faintly pink wine made from red grapes, popular in Alsace and Lorraine with luncheon dishes.

Vinho generoso [*vee*-nyo zheh-ne-*roh*-so]
Portuguese for fortified wine.

Vinho verde [*vee*-nyo *vair*-dee]
Literally, "green wine," actually young red, white or pink wines produced in the north of Portugal and drunk everywhere.

Vini di Lusso [*vee*-nee dee *loos*-so]
Italian expression for superior wines.

Vini tipici [*vee*-nee *tee*-pee-chee]
Literally, "typed wines," meaning recognized wines that have been popular for a long time, and are recognized as being distinctive. The government sets minimum standards for such wines, which are marketed with a red neck seal.

Vino corriente [*vee*-no cor-*yehn*-teh]
"Running wine," in Spanish, a term for ordinary wines.

Vin ordinaire [van nor-dee-nair]
The French term for sound wines with no particular distinction, the kind most frequently drunk all over Europe.

Volnay [vul-nay]
Large township of Burgundy's Côte de Beaune, producing soft, fruity wines excellent with meat and fowl.

Vöslau [*feus*-low]
One of the top Austrian wine districts, producing good reds and whites not often exported.

Vosne-Romanée [vohn-roh-ma-nay]
Town boasting the most famous group of Burgundy vineyards, velvety, rich wines for meats with sauces, game, poultry and wildfowl. Vineyards include Romanée-Conti, La Romanée, Romanée-St. Vivant, La Tâche, and Richebourg.

Vouvray [voo-vray]
Lightly sweet still or sparkling wine from this Loire district is made from the Chénin Blanc, and is good with fat foods, fish, and sea food.

Wachenheim [*vock*-en-hime]
Top Rheinpfalz township noted for its full-bodied wines of great finesse, from such vineyards as Gerumpel and Goldbachel. Excellent with smoked ham or fish, delicatessen, or fish, meat, or fowl served with white sauces.

Wachstum [*vox*-toom]
German meaning "growth," followed by the grower's name, and signifying an estate-bottling.

Wehlen [*vay*-len]
Top Mosel township, whose fruity but delicate wines command the highest prices of any Mosel, and are worth it, the fine vineyards including Sonnenuhr and Lay. Excellent by themselves, and with fish, sea food, and meats or fowl served with light sauces.

Weinberg [*vine*-bairg]
German for vineyard.

White Pinot
California name for wines made from the Pineau de la Loire, often good, to serve with fish, sea food, dishes with light sauces.

Wiltingen [*vil*-ting-en]
Leading Saar township, whose top vineyards include the *Scharzberg* (see) and Scharzhofberg.

Winkel [*vink*-el]
Top Rheingau township, whose most famous vineyard is *Schloss Vollrads*, which see.

Würzburg [*vürts*-boorg]
Top township of Franconia, famous for the hill known as the Stein. Würzburger Stein is fresh and flowery, a blend of Riesling, Sylvaner, and Traminer, and known as *Steinwein*, a name that has become the one used for *Frankenwein* all over the region. Good by themselves, with fish or delicatessen.

Xérès [zay-race]
French name for Spanish Sherry.

Yquem
Many people consider this famous Sauternes the greatest sweet white wine in the world. Luscious, fruity, and perfectly balanced, it is a wine to drink with desserts, or by itself. See *Bordeaux*.

Yvorne [ee-vorn]
Good light Swiss white wine from the Rhône, excellent with fish and sea food.

Zeltingen [*tsel*-ting-en]
Top wine town of the Mosel, producing one of the biggest and longest-lived of the region's wines, top vineyards including Schlossberg and Sonnenuhr. Superb with fish and sea food, ham and delicatessen, meat or fowl served with light sauces.

Zinfandel [*zin*-fan-del]
California red wine grape that produces hearty, full wines, the best of which come from Napa, Sonoma, and Santa Cruz. Like Beaujolais, excellent with roasts and stews.

Zucco [*tsook*-ko]
Sicilian sweet white wine, good with desserts.

Zwicker [tsvick-er]
Cheap blend of Alsatian wines.

F O O D S

The language of food, like that of love and diplomacy, is French, but this traditional pattern is changing now that regional dishes are becoming internationally known. The classic cuisine of palace hotels and starred restaurants continues to be described in French terms. Such dishes are compositions, varied by the various chefs, the materials carefully joined to augment or supplement one another. These traditional dishes are features of every good menu, but restaurants now tend to feature national and regional dishes as well. Such dishes are listed in the index, along with wines that bring out their flavors. The classic garnishes—nearly two hundred of them—and many of the classic sauces—over one hundred fifty of them—are listed separately, for quick reference. Various kinds and cuts of meat, fowl, fish, and sea food are listed under their French or national names, with the most popular ways of preparing them, and wines to go with them.

As the index was being prepared, it became apparent that a

cook only slightly familiar with the elements of cookery could use the book to prepare dishes and menus, but the main purpose of the index is to make possible the ordering of food in any good restaurant, anywhere. The phonetic spellings, which annoy some people, were included so that the reader would have some idea of how the words were pronounced; such spelling is often personal and whimsical, but the approximations are meant to help. It is hoped that they do.

Beef and game taste best with full red wines like Côte de Nuits Burgundies, Rhônes, and St. Émilions of Bordeaux. Simply broiled or roasted meats taste fine with lighter red wines like Bordeaux from Graves or the Médoc, with Côte de Beaune Burgundies.

Fowl tastes best with light reds of Bordeaux, although duck, wildfowl, and well-seasoned fowl dishes call for fuller reds like Burgundies or fruity ones like those of the Rhône or northern Italy. Whites of Burgundy or the Rhine are often served.

Veal and pork taste best with light reds, although much seasoning calls for full Burgundies and Rhônes.

Fish and sea food call for dry white Burgundies, although fat, smoked, or spicy dishes seem to go best with flowery wines of Graves, the Loire, the Rhine or the Moselle.

Stews and hearty dishes call for full reds like Burgundies or Rhônes, or beer.

Creamy dishes or those with light sauces call for light reds like Bordeaux, or fresh young reds like Beaujolais, *rosé* wines, or full dry Burgundy whites.

Spicy dishes taste best with full, dry Burgundy whites, *rosé* wines, or dry Sherries. Not only ham and delicatessen, but Oriental dishes, call for such wines, or for beer.

Names of dishes

Dishes are most frequently named after the place of origin, the garnish, or the sauce served with them. *Bœuf Bourguignon,* *steak au poivre,* and *tournedos béarnaise* are examples. Others are named after the method of cooking, a distinctive ingredient, or persons—sometimes the inventor, sometimes the inspirer.

And some have nicknames. *Bœuf braisé* is braised beef, *entre-côte Escoffier* is a way of preparing steak first done by that famous chef, and *pêche Melba* is named after the famous singer who so adored whipped cream that she was forced to diet on dry toast, which also came to be named for her. *Bubble and squeak* is the English name for sausages and mashed potatoes. Dishes are also named after the sort of person who might like them, like *omelette chasseur,* hunter's omelet, which contains chicken livers and mushrooms. The book is designed to make it possible to find your way through any menu in any good restaurant on earth. But note that when the name is geographical, although this may signify a particular ingredient, it may also mean simply the way the dish is cooked in that region. A dish designated "bourguignon" usually means that red wine was used in its making, although *escargots bourguignon* just means snails with garlic butter, the way they are prepared in Burgundy. Such exceptions are not particularly frequent. Wine suggestions are always a personal matter, subject to endless variation.

Index
of Foods

Aalsuppe [ahl-*zoop*-puh]
This Hamburg classic calls for simmering eel in a stock laced with lemon or white wine, then placing the pieces, with pears poached in white wine, in the bottom of a dish, combining the

stock with another of bouillon containing spinach, peas, and herbs, and pouring this into the bowl. Serve with Rhine wines.

Abatis de volaille [ah-bah-tee duh vo-leye]
Giblets braised or stewed in various ways, served on toast or rice, or with a garniture. *Chipolata* (chee-poh-*lah*-ta) is browned and garnished with tiny onions, chestnuts and diced bacon, surrounded with tiny sausages; *à la bourguignonne* is browned with diced onions and bacon, then moistened with red wine and brown stock and served with tiny onions and more bacon, the whole sprinkled with parsley. German versions often boil or blanch the giblets, stew them with fruit, and serve them with dumplings. Serve with hearty red wines like Burgundies or Rhônes.

Abbacchio [ahb-*bok*-kyo]
Suckling lamb roasted in the oven or on the spit, although Romans also serve it cut up, *alla cacciatore* (kach-chah-*tor*-reh), sautéed with rosemary, garlic, pepper, vinegar, and anchovies, or *brodettato* (broh-deht-*taht*-toh) in a casserole with ham, marjoram, chopped onion, and parsley, with a mixture of beaten eggs and lemon juice. Serve with local wines like the white Frascati, or with a full-bodied wine like Barolo or Chianti.

Agneau de lait de Provence [ahn-yo duh lay duh pro-vahns]
Suckling lamb roasted on the spit, after being basted with oil and mashed juniper, is a spring classic often served with a pink wine like Tavel, or a fruity red like Beaujolais or Châteauneuf-du-Pape.

Agnello al forno [ahn-*yehl*-lo ahl *for*-no]
Roast legs of lamb rubbed with garlic, sprinkled with rosemary, and roasted in lard with quartered potatoes. Serve with local Italian red wines like Barolo or Chianti.

Agnollotti alla piemontese [ahn-yo-*lot*-tee ahl-lah pyeh-mawn-*teh*-zeh]
A mixture of sausage and chopped beef and pork, with cabbage moistened with Marsala or egg, and bound with bread crumbs,

stuffed into *pasta* squares like those called ravioli, and served with a sprinkling of Parmesan cheese. Serve with Nebbiolo or other Piedmontese red wine.

Albóndigas con guisantes [ahl-*bohn*-dee-gahs con ghee-*sahn*-tehs] Spanish meatballs, usually of chopped beef, ham, and onions, browned, then simmered in a tomato sauce, in which green peas are mixed for serving. Serve with red or white Rioja.

Alicot [ah-lee-ko]
This Gascon stew of goose, chicken, or duck giblets with chopped onions, tomatoes, and ham, simmered in bouillon with a *bouquet garni*, is often confused with *aligot*, which is diced cheese added to potatoes fried with garlic, and with *haricot de mouton* (ar-ree-koh duh moo-tawn) which is a mutton stew with turnips, onions, and potatoes. All are best served with reds like Burgundy.

Alose de Loire grillée [ah-lohz duh lwahr gree-yay]
Shad, that glory of spring, marinated in Vouvray and lemon juice, then sprinkled with olive oil, grilled, and served with slices of fried roe, a sorrel purée, and a Vouvray sauce. Serve with Vouvray, Muscadet or other light or flowery white wine. *Farcie à l'angevine* (far-see ah lahnzh-van) is stuffed with roe, which is often mashed with sorrel and nutmeg, then bound with butter and egg, after which it is baked with chopped shallots in dry white Anjou; *grillée à l'oseille* (greel-lay ah loh-zehy) is stuffed with roe and chopped sorrel, browned, dipped in olive oil, and grilled; *à la valentinoise* (va-lahn-teen-wahz) is first

simmered on a bed of chopped sorrel, onions, and shallots, then soaked in brandy and dry white wine, and baked: *à la piquerette* (peek-ret) is stewed shad in Anjou, with chopped garlic, onions, and parsley, the sauce being thickened with butter and crumbs.

Alouette à la bonne femme   [ah-loo-et ah lah bon fam]
Larks are a French delicacy, and when done housewife's style they are roasted with crumbled bacon, then a little brandy is poured over the birds, which are served with croutons. Larks *à l'anglaise* (lahn-glehz) and *à la provençale* (proh-vahn-sal) are also roasted, the first with butter and parsleyed bread crumbs, the second with mushrooms, olives, and tomato paste with garlic; *sans tête* (sahn tet) are veal rolls stuffed with ground meat, garlic, and parsley. Serve with red Burgundy, Rhône, or other full red wine.

Aloyau de bœuf   [ah-loy-oh duh buhf]
The sirloin of beef, usually roasted, served with red wines.

Aloyau de bœuf aux primeurs   [ah-loy-yo duh beuf oh pree-meurs]
The sirloin of beef—the loin and tenderloin—served with spring vegetables. Invariably roasted, it is served with the same garnitures used for the tenderloin: *à la bretonne* (breh-ton) is served with white beans; *à la bourgeoise* (boor-zhwahz) with glazed onions, carrots, and crumbled bacon; *à la française* (frahn-sehz) with spinach tartlets and *pommes Anna* (pom-zahn-nah). Serve with red Bordeaux, Burgundy, Rhône, or local red wines.

Amourettes   [ah-moor-ets]
Poached beef marrow, generally diced and mixed with a sauce and mushrooms or truffles, then breaded and fried. Accompanied with red wines such as Burgundy.

Anchoïade languedocienne   [ahn-shoy-ahd lahng-dohs-yen]
Fresh anchovy fillets dipped in batter and fried with garlic and laurel, then served with chopped onions. Accompany with Provence whites or *rosés*.

Anguille au vert   [ahn-ghee oh vair]
Eels are a Flemish and Belgian specialty, in this case simmered

on a bed of sorrel, lettuce, and beets previously simmered with beer and butter; *à la bière* (byair) is even more popular, generally baby eels (elvers) lightly sautéed in butter, then soaked in a beer and yolk batter, and further simmered in beer, then served on fried toast; *à la gelée* (zhuh-lay) is eels cooked in wine and bouillon with onions and mushrooms, and served cold in the jellied bouillon. Serve with beer or schnapps.

Animelle [ah-nee-*mehl*-leh]
Sweetbreads, fried with ham. Serve with a dry white wine, like Soave.

Anitra selvatica in salmì [*ah*-nee-trah sehl-*vah*-tee-kah een sahl-*mee*]
Wild duck stewed in a casserole with butter and oil, in a sauce of the giblets, onions and parsley, orange juice and red wine. Serve with hearty red wines like Barolo.

Annegati [ahn-neh-*gah*-ti]
Skewered veal chunks stewed in white wine, a Milanese specialty that tastes fine with a Valtellina, red or white.

Arista [*ah*-rees-tah]
Loin of pork roasted on the spit or in the oven with rosemary and garlic. Serve with any dry white wine, like Verdicchio or Orvieto, or with a light red wine, like Bardolino or Chianti.

Arrostino annegato alla milanese [ah-ros-*tee*-no ahn-neh-*gah*-to *ahl*-lah mee-lah-*nay*-zeh]
Browned veal loin wrapped around strips of calf's liver, sliced and skewered, seasoned with sage and rosemary, then stewed in white wine and brown stock laced with lemon juice, glazed in the oven, and served with *risotto* and the pan gravy. Serve with Barolo, Gattinara, or other mature roast wines.

Arroz a la alicantina [ah-*roth* ah lah ah-lee-kon-*tee*-nah]
Saffron rice with fish, peas, and artichokes, seasoned with garlic, tomato, and pepper. Alicante specialty, along with "ali-oli," the oil and garlic sauce used with fish. Serve with dry white Rioja or Alella.

Arroz a la valenciana [ah-*roth* ah lah vah-lehn-thee-*ah*-nah]
What most people think of as *paella valenciana*, saffron rice
with chicken and sea food, with mussels or clams, sausage,
pimiento and peas. Lobster, shrimp, lean pork, octopus, and
string beans or artichokes are often included, along with tomatoes. Serve with red or white Rioja, a dry Sherry such as Manzanilla, or Montilla.

Arroz con mejillones [ah-*roth* con meh-heel-yo-nehs]
Saffron rice cooked in a fish broth that includes carrots and
onion, with shelled mussels, finished in an earthenware pot in
the oven. Lugo specialty. Serve with dry white Rioja.

Arroz parellada [ar-*roth* pah-rehl-*yah*-do]
Pieces of chicken, fish and sea food sautéed in the large flat pan
called a *paellera* (pah-el-*yair*-ah) with artichokes, sweet peppers, and peas, seasoned with diced tomato, onion, and garlic,
which is then arranged in a mold, with a mound of boiled rice
on a bed of mushrooms, the whole finished in the oven, then
sprinkled with parsley. Gerona specialty, with *pollo al espetón*
(*pol*-yo ahl es-peh-*tohn*), chicken broiled on a spit. Serve with
young red or white dry Rioja.

Aspic à la gauloise [ah-speek ah lah gohl-wahz]
Molds of chilled gelatine containing various vegetables, meats,
fowl, fish, and game are delicate luncheon dishes or fancy
courses for a banquet or buffet, the Gaulish one containing
chicken breasts and cocks' kidneys and combs coated with a
white sauce and arranged with slices of truffle; *à la banquière*
(bahnk-yair) substitutes *foie gras* and slices of egg white and
mushrooms for the chicken; aspics of fish usually contain diced
vegetables. Serve with dry or flowery white wines of Burgundy,
the Loire, or the Rhineland, or Champagne.

Bacalao a la vizcaina   [bah-kah-*lah*-oh ah lah veeth-cah-*ee*-nah]
Pieces of boiled cod are floured, then sautéed in oil; a sauce of
onions, garlic, tomatoes, and peppers, seasoned with thyme, is
sautéed with bread, and the dish is finished by placing the cod
on strips of roasted red peppers, pouring the sauce over, roasting for a few minutes in the oven, then garnishing with fried
bread slices. This Basque dish is eaten with red or white wine,
preferably Rioja.

Baccalà   [bahk-kah-*lah*]
Dried salt cod, soaked in water then cooked in various ways, is
as much an Italian favorite as it is Spanish and Portuguese; *alla
bolognese* (bo-lo-*nyeh*-zeh) is with an oil-and-butter sauce
seasoned with parsley, garlic, and pepper; *alla fiorentina* (fyor-
en-*tee*-nah) is floured then cooked in a casserole in oil, salt,
and pepper; *alla napolitana* (nah-pol-ee-*tah*-nah) is floured then
sautéed and stuffed with black olives, capers, tomatoes, and
garlic; *alla romana* (ro-*mah*-nah) is sautéed in oil with pine
nuts, onions, and tomatoes, while *alla vicenza* (vee-*chen*-tsah)
adds minced anchovies, cinnamon, garlic, and parsley, the pieces
dipped in milk; *alla Venezia* (ve-*nehts*-ya) is browned in oil
and butter with onions, then cooked in milk or Béchamel with
anchovies, but the Venetians also like the cod *mantecato*
(mahn-teh-*kah*-to) or frothed, the cod being boiled in oil, and
whipped. Serve with any wine, preferably a full, dry white like
Soave.

Backhendl   [*bahk*-hehn-dl]
A Viennese specialty, breaded chicken quarters deep fried, garnished with fried parsley and served with a cucumber salad,
roast potatoes. Serve with Austrian whites like Gumpoldskirch-
ner.

Ballottine d'agneau braisée   [bahl-loht-teen dahn-yo bray-zay]
A sort of galantine, generally served hot, made by stuffing a
boned lamb shoulder with sausage meat, chopped onions, and
parsley, trussing it well, then braising the ball or loaf in stock.
Pork and veal shoulders and boned fowl are prepared in similar

fashion, and served with a variety of garnishes. Serve hot with a good red Bordeaux or estate-bottled Burgundy, or with a dry white like Pouilly-Fuissé when cold.

Bar [bahr]
Sea bass, often served cold when boiled or poached, but more often braised, fried, grilled, or sautéed, served with various sauces, and white wines like Graves.

Barbeau [bar-boh]
Barbel is a freshwater fish, generally boiled or grilled; in Périgord it is poached in white-wine bouillon, which is reduced and mixed with brown butter to make a sauce; in the Touraine it is marinated in olive oil and brandy, then poached in Chinon, with herbs, and served on toast with buttered mushrooms, and the stock mixed with cream. Serve with dry white or *rosé* wines of the Loire or Provence.

Barbue [bar-bü]
Brill is a salt-water bottom fish, something like turbot, served in filets, and generally baked or braised, although stuffed brill is poached. Serve with any dry or flowery white wine, like Graves or Meursault.

Baron of beef
An English classic, traditionally paraded around the banquet hall on a wooden plank carried by four Beefeaters before being carved, the baron consists of two sirloins of beef still joined together and roasted over an open fire. Lamb and mutton are prepared in the same way, but do not require a tour of Beefeaters. A Côte d'Or red Burgundy or English ale is drunk with this.

Bayerische Leberknödel [*by*-er-ih-shuh lay-ber-*kneu*-del]
The famous liver dumplings of Bavaria, poached, then served with black butter and sauerkraut. Serve with dark German beer or a full Riesling from the Rheinpfalz or the Rheingau.

Bécasse farcie [bay-kahs far-see]
Woodcock—stuffed with its chopped giblets, bacon, parsley,

chives, and butter—skewered and grilled or roasted, then served on toast. Serve with red wines like Burgundy or St. Émilion.

Beef

The most popular of meats, the best beef probably comes from Japan, where the steer, or ox, is fed beer and given a daily rubdown to make its flanks tender. French beef from the Charolles is much admired, and good words are said of Argentine and Texas beef, the quality depending on breed and feed, range and care, age and aging. The tenderest cuts are from the sirloin, called *aloyau* in French, between the ribs and the rump, or round. The sirloin proper is the larger cut across the loin, the undercut being called the tenderloin. In France, these are called the *contre-filet* (kohn-truh fee-lay) or *faux filet* (foh), and the *filet*. The French cuts of the filet are, starting from the rump end; *bifteck* (our tenderloin steak), *châteaubriand*, *filet, tournedos*, and *filet mignon* (mee-nyawn) the steaks getting smaller around and tenderer. The ribs, or *train de côte* (tran duh koht) provide the steak called *entrecôte* (ahn-truh-koht) while the round provides *romsteck* (rohm-stek). Our porterhouse steak, also called T-bone, which includes the sirloin, bone, and tenderloin, is not found in French butchery. Steaks cooked very rare—still purplish in the center—are termed *bleu* in French, while rare steaks—blood-red in the center—are called *sangnant* (sahn-nyahn). They are generally grilled, sautéed, or braised. They are served with red wines, the delicate cuts often calling for light Bordeaux, while the heartier steaks call for the fuller Burgundies and Rhônes, particularly when spicy sauces are served with them.

Beignets [bain-yay]

Fritters, some of the most unusual being the Norman oyster fritters, the snail fritters of Provence that are cooked in a spicy bouillon, *beignets de poutina* (duh poo-tee-nah) which are whitebait fritters of Nice, and *beignets d'oseille* (doh-zehy), which are sorrel leaves dipped in batter and fried, served in Périgord with fowl and game. Serve with white wines.

Bifteck
The tenderloin or filet steak, generally grilled or sautéed, and
served with many different garnishes, accompanied with red
Burgundies.

Bistecca alla fiorentina [bee-*stehk*-kah]
Cutlets of Tuscan veal or steak, sliced thin, and grilled without
additional fat, seasoned only with salt and pepper. This
gloriously simple dish is best with young, fruity red Chianti.

Bistecca alla pizzaiola [bee-*stehk*-kah *ahl*-lah peets-sy-*oh*-lah]
Very thin slices of beef rump or filet, beaten still thinner, salted
and peppered, sautéed in hot oil, then bathed in a tomato and
oregano sauce seasoned with garlic, salt, and pepper. Serve with
full reds like Barolo or Chianti.

Blanquette de veau [blahn-ket duh voh]
The classic of French *cuisine bourgeoise*—ranking with *pot-au-
feu* and *bœuf bourguignon*—blanched veal fricassée, served in
white sauce. Also done with chicken and lamb. Serve with light
reds like Beaujolais.

Blaulachs [blow-lox]
Salmon—particularly the famous *Rheinsalm* (*ryn*-zahlm)—
trout, eel, carp, and other fish, are frequently served "blue" in
Germany, which involves plunging the fish into simmering wine
or vinegar or fish stock that has been seasoned with herbs, thus
bringing out the desired hue. The fish poaches quickly in the
liquid, and is usually served with boiled potatoes or other simply cooked vegetables, and Rhine wines.

Bolitas españolas [bo-*lee*-tahs es-pan-*yo*-lahs]
Spanish meat dumplings, sautéed in oil, then stewed in a mixture of *sauce madère* and tomato sauce. More delicate than
albóndigas. Serve with red Rioja.

Il bollito [eel bohl-*lee*-toh]
A platter of various boiled meats—beef, veal heads, veal hocks
—served in the Piedmont with *salsa verde* (*sahl*-sah *vair*-deh),
a classic Italian sauce of oil, vinegar, capers and parsley. Serve
with any light red or white wine, like Valtellina.

Bouchées [boo-shay]
These are baked rounds of pastry filled with various rich or
creamy fillings, although *bouchées à la Pauillac* (poh-ee-yak)
are fried potato croquettes stuffed with chopped ham and other
meats, mixed with chives and bound with yolk, then baked.
Serve with light wines like Médoc or Graves.

Boudin blanc [boo-dan blahn]
This holiday sausage which is eaten the year around—and
generally listed under *charcuterie*, products of the pork butcher
meant to precede a meal—often becomes a luncheon dish
when accompanied with vegetables. This "white pudding" is
filled with creamed chicken breast along the Loire, with bread
elsewhere. Like *boudin noir* (nwahr), blood pudding, it is
served with white wines like Vouvray or Anjou.

Bouillabaisse [boo-yah-behss]
The classic fish soup of Marseilles, imitated everywhere, but
depending for its excellence on local rockfish like *rascasse* and
rouget, and, often, *langouste*. The various fish are quickly
boiled in water or stock containing saffron, garlic, and herbs,
olive oil and tomatoes. For serving, the bouillon is poured over
bread in a bowl, the fish served separately. Accompany with
Provence whites or *rosés*.

Bouillade [boo-yahd]
Sometimes called *bouillonnade*, or *bouillabaisse catalane*, a fish
stew that includes mussels, the fish being served on garlic toast
with a sauce of pimiento and browned chopped garlic sautéed
in oil, to which flour and white wine is added. Serve with beer
or local dry white wine.

Brandade [brahn-dod]
This Provençal specialty is a classic of peasant cooking; dried cod is soaked then scalded, after which, still hot, it is pounded in a mortar with warm milk and mashed garlic, nutmeg, and lemon juice, olive oil being added drop by drop, then spooned on croutons fried in olive oil and set in a very hot dish. Accompany with Provence whites or *rosés*. A Languedoc version, *brandade de morue* (moh-rü) is garnished with truffles.

Brème aux onions [brem oh-zohn-yawn]
Along the upper Loire, bream is laid on a bed of minced onions, doused with white wine, and braised with parsley and thyme; as *brème farci grand'mère*, it is stuffed with milk-soaked crumbs and melted butter, chopped mushrooms, onions, and parsley, nutmeg and beaten egg, and baked in white wine and more butter. *Brème à la mode* is marinated in oil and herbs, then grilled and covered with a white wine sauce that includes mustard, chopped shallots, and parsley, thickened with butter and yolk. This fish calls for flowery whites like Pouilly-Fumé or Sylvaner.

Broade [bro-*ah*-deh]
Turnips that have soured and fermented with pulp of fresh grapes, sliced and sautéed with bacon, sausage, onions, and parsley. Serve with a dry white wine like Soave or Orvieto.

Brochet à la broche [bro-sheh ah lah brawsh]
Pike is a French favorite, particularly in Burgundy, where it is skewered, sprinkled with a butter-and-Chablis sauce, then grilled and served with *sauce dijonnais*—yolk, butter, and mustard. When braised or roasted, sole and turbot garnishes are used. Serve with Chablis.

Brodetto di pesce [broh-*deht*-to dee *peh*-sheh]
A brothy stew of local fish, particularly celebrated in Trieste, Venice, and other port cities. Serve with local white wines, like dry Soave.

Brouillade aux truffes [broo-yahd oh trüf]
Eggs scrambled with chopped truffles.

Burrida [boor-*ree*-dah]
Famous Genoese bouillabaisse, that includes pine nuts, celery, and parsley, in addition to saffron and other seasonings, the broth served in a bowl separate from the fish. Serve with any dry or flowery white wine, such as Cinque Terre or Soave.

Cabri en sauce [kah-bree on sohs]
Kid is a Corsican specialty when braised in bouillon and served with a thick red wine sauce enriched with tomato and garlic, chopped onion and parsley; or when chunks are barbecued over a wood fire and basted with oil and vinegar; or when the shoulder is stuffed with pork, veal, liver, and spinach, all bound with egg. Often served with *la polenta di castagne* (kah-*stahn*-yeh) made with chestnut flour. Serve with local reds or Rhônes.

Cacciucco [kach-*chook*-ko]
A glorious fish stew with red wine, served on garlic toast. Serve with any dry white wine, like Orvieto, or a light red like Bardolino.

"La Cachelada" [lah kah-cheh-*lah*-dah]
A ragout of potatoes and *chorizos* (choh-*ree*-thohs), these hot sausages being boiled, then large pieces of potato being added and cooked until they are done. León specialty, along with *"truchas con unto"* (*troo*-chahs kon *oon*-to), sautéed trout with bacon. Serve with red or white Rioja.

Cachelos [kah-*cheh*-los]
A boiled dinner, made by boiling cabbage with sausages and ham hocks, then mixing the cabbage with boiled potatoes in a casserole, and sautéing these with bacon, red pepper, and garlic. The meat is served in a separate dish. Specialty of La Coruña, along with *la calderada* (kahl-deh-*rah*-dah), a kind of stew; *empanada de "Xouba"* (em-pa-*nah*-da deh *shoo*-bah), a meat pie. A fruity red wine, a young Rioja or Valdepeñas, is the classic accompaniment.

Cailles sous la cendre [ky-yuh soo lah son-druh]
Quail cooked in the ashes, wrapped in vine leaves and buttered

paper, but first stuffed with chopped bacon, chicken livers, truffles, and *foie gras*, with seasonings, and bound with brandy. Serve with full red Burgundies like Nuits-St.-Georges.

Les Caillettes   [lay ky-yet]
These "little quail" are pig's livers chopped with parsley, spinach, and other herbs, wrapped in skin, and baked. Serve hot or cold with Pouilly-Fumé or other dry white wine.

Calderata asturiana   [kahl-deh-*rah*-tah ah-stoo-ree-*ah*-na]
Fish and shellfish stew prepared in a deep pot, first boiled in water seasoned with red pepper, chopped onion, oil and salt. After the boiling has begun, nutmeg, crushed sweet pepper, a cayenne pod and a cup of dry Sherry are added. Oviedo specialty, along with *fabada asturiana* (fah-*bah*-dah), Iberian pork and beans that includes potatoes, cabbage, and corned beef, as well as other parts of the pig. Serve with dry or flowery white Rioja.

Calderata extremeña   [kahl-deh-*rah*-tah es-treh-*may*-nya]
Lamb pot roast, seasoned with red peppers and laurel and the local red wine, and spiced with a concentrated sauce made of the lamb liver, garlic, and black pepper. Serve with local wine or young red Rioja.

Caldo de pescado   [*kahl*-do deh pehs-*kah*-do]
A fish soup, mainly potatoes and sea bream or sea pike, flavored with tomatoes, onions, saffron, and cumin, boiled in an earthenware pot and served over thin slices of bread set in the soup plates. Santa Cruz specialty, but there are versions in every seaport along the Mediterranean.

Callos a la madrileña   [*kahl*-yose ah lah mah-dree-*lay*-nya]
Tripe is a Spanish favorite, and this Madrid specialty is a classic,
pieces being boiled in wine and water laced with lemon, together with calf's feet and a *bouquet garni*, the water then being changed and the tripe being brought to a boil again, with
more wine and brandy being added, along with peppers and a
new *bouquet*. When tender, chopped onion and ham, sausage
slices and Plasencia pepper, are used as seasoning. Stews and
roast suckling pigs are also Madrid specialties. Serve with fruity
young or old Rioja.

Canard rouennaise   [kah-nar roo-ahn-nehz]
The best duck comes from Rouen, and this classic Norman
way of preparing it is to roast it halfway, then cut strips from
the carcass, sprinkle these with minced shallots and flame them
with Cognac, and serve with the grilled drumsticks, a rich
sauce being made from the blood and pressed carcass. Ducks
are roasted and braised in various ways, but all call for a full
red wine like Côte d'Or Burgundy.

Caneton St. Martin de Tours   [kah-nuh-ton san mar-tan duh
toor]
Duckling cooked in a pig's bladder in veal stock, served with
candied chestnuts and a sauce made of the stock, Vouvray, and
orange juice. In Nantes, roast duckling is served with peas, new
onions, and bacon; and throughout Normandy, in the pan
juices mixed with the liver and cream. Serve with full red
Burgundies.

Cannelloni   [kan-nehl-*loh*-nee]
Every restaurant has its own version, a *pasta* case stuffed with
minced meat or fish and served with a thin tomato or meat
sauce. Serve with any dry white wine, like Frascati, or a light
red like Bardolino.

Caponata   [kah-po-*nah*-tah]
Hard biscuits covered with sliced onions and tomatoes, anchovies, green peppers or eggplant, garlic and basil, soaked with

oil and vinegar, generally served as a sort of salad with simply cooked meats or cold cuts. Serve with a dry white wine, like Orvieto, or a light red wine like Bardolino.

Cappon magro [kahp-*pohn mah*-gro]
Called the queen of salads, this is Genoese, a pyramid made of layers of hard biscuits rubbed with garlic and spread with anchovy paste spiced with mashed olives and capers, parsley, pine nuts, and egg yolk, with slices of cold boiled vegetables, the whole drenched with oil and vinegar and topped with pieces of boiled fish, lobster, and other sea food in a green sauce. Serve with any dry white wine, like Orvieto, or even the intense Vernaccia.

Capretto al forno [kah-*preht*-to ahl *for*-no]
Roast kid is a Sicilian favorite, popular elsewhere when suckling pig isn't available, generally roasted whole and redolent with herbs. Serve with Etna or other full red wines.

Carbonnade [kar-bawn-nod]
Formerly, a *carbonnade* was any grilled meat, but now the name applies mostly to thin strips of beef or pork that are grilled. *Carbonnades à la flamande* are browned beef slices put in a casserole with minced onion layers, covered with beer, and baked in the oven. A famous specialty of Languedoc is rump steak, diced and browned with a mince of onions and tomatoes, then braised with rice and corn, saffron and pimiento, spiced with brown sugar and cinnamon, the whole moistened with white wine. Serve with beer or Rhône reds.

Carpe farcie à l'alsacienne [carp far-see ah lahl-sah-syen]
This version of one of France's favorite fish, a sort of Alsatian *gefüllte fisch* (ghuh-*fil*-tuh fish), is carp stuffed with mashed fish in cream, then poached in white wine. Because of its firmness and pronounced flavor, carp is prepared almost like meat —grilled, braised, and in stews. Serve with full whites like Traminer or Meursault, or Côte de Beaune reds.

Carré d'agneau [kar-ray dah-nyo]
That part of the suckling lamb between the shoulder and the
saddle, which is usually grilled on a spit, braised, or roasted:
à la beauharnais (boh-ar-neh) is grilled over a slow fire, finally
sprinkled with bread crumbs and browned over a fast fire, then
served with new potatoes, and buttered artichoke hearts filled
with *sauce beauharnais*, the whole sauced with *demi-glace* and
melted butter.

Carré de porc rôti à la provençale [kar-ray duh por roh-tee ah
lah proh-vahn-sal]
Pork is usually pricked with garlic, but in Provence sage is used,
the meat is rubbed with salt, thyme, and laurel, then marinated
in olive oil and garlic, and finally roasted with garlic. Serve with
red Rhônes or *rosés*.

Cassoulet [kahs-soo-lay]
The pot of white beans is a glory of southern France that once
varied infinitely from cook to cook, who added anything to the
bean pot on the back of the stove. Today the three most famous
cassoulets are: *Castelnaudary* (kah-stel-noh-dah-ree), which contains bits of preserved pork browned in goose fat, and country
sausage with a brown sauce, mixed with the beans, and finally
sprinkled with crumbs and parsley; *Carcassonne* (kar-kah-son)
is similar, but the beans are first stewed with sausage, garlic and
carrots, the preserved pork is browned with pork chops and
mashed garlic, and other meats are added; *Toulouse* adds leg of
mutton instead of pork chops, and tomatoes. Serve with
Rhône reds or whites, or beer.

Catalane [ka-tah-lan]
The French versions of dishes from northern Spain, usually
denoting plenty of garlic, and cooking in oil.

Cazuela a la catalana [kah-*thweh*-la ah la kah-ta-*lah*-na]
Diced beef or veal browned in oil in an earthenware pot, the
fat being used to sauté onion, tomato, and carrot. The meat is

returned to the pot, with thyme and water, for simmering, then slices of sausage are added, the dish being finished in the oven. Lérida specialty, along with Léridan peas. Serve with red Rioja.

Cazuela de habas verdes   [kah-*thweh*-la deh *ah*-bahs *vair*-dehs]
Stew of green beans with artichokes, flavored with saffron, mint, and laurel, each serving topped with a poached egg. Granada specialty, along with *empanadillas* (em-pah-nah-*deel*-yahs) *de Santa Catalina,* meat tarts, and Trévelez ham. Serve with white Rioja.

Cêpes farcies aux escargots   [sep far-see oh zes-kar-go]
These mushrooms are popular everywhere in France, but one of the most typical of specialties is this Burgundian way of stuffing them with the chopped mushroom stalks, and snails that have been simmered in Meursault; this wine is served with them. They are also grilled and sautéed, the stalks chopped and mixed with garlic and parsley, occasionally crumbs, then browned; *à la bordelaise* is the way of sautéing them in olive oil, with shallots, parsley, and garlic. Generally served with red wines like Graves or Médoc.

Cerdo asado a la riojana   [*thair*-do ah-*sah*-do ah lah ree-oh-*hah*-na]
Pork roasted in an open oven, well rubbed with garlic, and served with fried whole pimientos. Rioja specialty, so serve with a red Rioja.

Cervelles en meurette   [sehr-vel on muhr-et]
Brains stewed in red Burgundy, along with a *bouquet garni* and chopped onions, carrots, and garlic, then served on toast with the thickened sauce, accompanied with a red Côte d'Or Burgundy.

Chanfaina [chon-fah-*ee*-nah]
Pieces of pig's liver sautéed in oil with onions, then stewed with chopped parsley and mint, with saffron, paprika, peppercorns, cinnamon, and cloves, and sprinkled with bread crumbs just before serving. This hearty dish calls for a young hearty Rioja.

Chartreuse de perdrix [shar-truhz duh pair-dree]
A *chartreuse*, named after the monastical order, means vegetables in a dish, not the liqueur. In this case cabbage forms a bed for browned partridge, along with bacon, chopped onions and carrots, ham and sausage, the whole covered with more cabbage leaves, sprinkled with bouillon, then baked. The Alsatian version is young partridges and braised cabbage baked in a mold that has been filled with a purée of the giblets, carrots, turnips, green beans, and Brussels sprouts. Serve with a red Burgundy.

Châteaubriand [shah-toh-bree-ahn]
A thick steak cut from the center of the tenderloin, served with a variety of sauces and garnishes, generally accompanied with full-bodied red wines such as St. Émilion or Burgundies.

Chaudrée [shoh-dray]
A slow-cooked fish stew, with garlic, onions, and cloves, in white wine. Serve with Graves or Muscadet.

Chipirones [chee-pee-*roh*-nehs]
A Basque casserole of inkfish, the cuttlefish called *calamare* (kah-lah-*mah*-reh), sautéed in olive oil with chopped onions and various other seasoning ingredients, including the ink. Serve with beer, or flowery whites like Graves.

Choucroute alsacienne [shoo-kroot ahl-sas-yen]
The sauerkraut of Alsace, cooked in white wine with juniper berries, in a pan lined with salt pork, carrots, and onions stuck with cloves, to which are often added smoked ham, pork, and brisket of beef, sausages, bacon, peppercorns, *foie gras*, and potatoes. Serve with beer, or Alsatian wines like Sylvaner or Traminer.

Cima di vitello alla genovese [*chee*-mah dee vee-*tehl*-lo ah-la jeh-no-*vay*-zeh]
Veal wrapped around chopped sweetbreads, brains and other meats, peas and artichokes, the filling bound with egg, the whole simmered in broth, and served hot or cold. Serve with a dry white wine, like Soave, or a light red wine like Bardolino.

Cipolle ripiene [chee-*pohl*-leh ree-*pyeh*-neh]
Onions stuffed with sausage, baked and served with grated parmigiano. Serve with Cortese, or other light white wine.

Civet de lièvre [see-vay duh lee-ev-ruh]
First catch your rabbit, goes the old recipe for this classic, which is a red-wine stew of jugged hare with bacon, onions, and mushrooms, the sauce thickened with giblets and blood, the whole flamed with Cognac. In Alsace, pork is used, in Normandy, crawfish. Because of the rich sauce, a light red wine like Médoc is a good choice, although Burgundy is traditional.

Cochinillo asado [co-chee-*neel*-yo ah-*sah*-do]
Roast suckling pig is one of the most classic Spanish dishes, the split carcass being thrust into roaring open ovens, the skin being dampened with brine until it blisters and turns golden. It is a particular specialty of Segovia, but many restaurants in Madrid and throughout the country feature this traditional glory of the roaster's art. Serve with a fresh young or fine old red Rioja, or a good red Burgundy or Bordeaux.

Cochon de lait à la bourguignonne [ko-shawn duh lay]
A Burgundian classic, roast suckling pig stuffed with chopped giblets, parsley, garlic, and sage, browned in fat, then mixed with white wine, to be served with Côte de Beaune reds like Corton or Volnay.

Cocido extremeño [co-*thee*-doh es-treh-*meh*-nyo]
Boiled meat stew, including chunks of beef, sausages, chicken, and bacon, with chickpeas, cabbage, and potatoes, in herb broth or with rice seasoned with peppermint, often served with a piquant tomato sauce. Badajoz specialty, along with *gazpacho*

(gahth-*pah-cho*) (cold vegetable soup), *chorizo emborrajado* (choh-*ree*-tho em-bor-rah-*hah*-do) (sausage with borage), and melons. Serve with red Rioja or Valdepeñas.

Colin [ko-lan]
This fish is called *merlan* (mehr-lahn) in Provence and *saumon blanc* (soh-mawn blahn) on many menus, and is pollack in English. It is often poached and served cold, with mayonnaise; a Basque specialty is to lay filets on chopped, browned green onions, allowing the fish to steam, then serving it on toast. Accompany with white Graves or Meursault.

Confits pyrénéens [kawn-fee pee-ray-nay-ahn]
Potted fowl or pork that has been pickled, larded with garlic, braised, then covered with melted lard. Served with bread and full red wines like Burgundies or Rhônes.

Coniglio in cartoccio [ko-*neel*-yo een kar-*toch*-cho]
Rabbit that has been marinated in oil with chopped garlic, onions, mushrooms, and parsley, then roasted in paper and served in the bag. Serve with light or full red wines, like Chianti or Barolo.

Contrefilet [kohn-truh-fee-lay]
The loin of beef, sometimes roasted whole, but usually cut in steaks and grilled, like sirloin steak. Accompany with red wines like Burgundies or Rhônes.

Copa [ko-pah]
La Copa is a Corsican specialty, roasted pork shoulder, rolled and skewered, stuffed with chopped forcemeat, spinach, and herbs, and served with local reds or Rhônes.

Coq au vin [kawk oh van]
Rooster parts browned with bacon, spring onions, and mushrooms, then flamed with brandy and stewed in red wine with garlic and a *bouquet garni*, generally served on toast, the sauce thickened with blood. Specialty in all red wine regions, particularly Burgundy, and served with the same wine used in stewing.

Coquilles Saint-Jacques   [ko-kee-yuh san-zhack]
In Brittany and elsewhere, chopped scallops with chopped onions, garlic, and parsley, moistened with white wine and crumbled, then baked in the shells. This dish is drowned in a cream sauce in Paris, usually with cheese, which destroys its delicacy. Serve with dry whites like Muscadet.

Cordero asado   [kor-*deh*-ro ah-*sah*-do]
Most simply, roast lamb, but often lamb chunks baked in an earthenware pan, to which a little red wine and lemon juice is added, just before the pan is taken from the oven. Logroño specialty, along with *perdriz en chocolate* (pair-*dreeth* en cho-ko-*lah*-teh), a similarly cooked partridge flavored with chocolate. Serve with young red Rioja.

Cordero en ajillo pastor   [kor-deh-ro en ah-*heel*-yo pahs-*tor*]
"Lamb with shepherd's garlic" is made by sautéing chunks of lamb with red peppers, then pouring over this a reduced sauce of mashed garlic, cumin, and saffron in white wine; served with fried potatoes. Jaen specialty, along with *pipirrana jaenera* (pee-pee-*rah*-na ha-en-*ehr*-rah), diced tomatoes, peppers, and hard-boiled egg whites, served with a garlic sauce and slices of ham. Accompany with fruity young red Rioja or medium-dry white Rioja.

Costata alla pizzaiuola   [koh-*stah*-tah *ahl*-lah peet-sy-*woh*-lah]
This Neapolitan specialty, veal or beef slices pounded very thin and quickly pan-broiled, is served with an aromatic sauce. Serve with red Gragnano or Vulture.

Côtelettes de veau à l'étouffée [cawt-let duh vo ah lay-toof-fay]
Veal cutlets browned with chopped bacon and onion, garlic and parsley, then braised in red or white wine; *morvandelle* (mor-vahn-del) calls for browning the cutlets with diced ham and spring onions, then braising in Pouilly-Fumé; *en poirée* calls for stuffing thick cutlets with chopped sweetbreads and pickled pork, parsley and chives, mushrooms and shallots, braised with bacon in white Burgundy and bouillon. Serve with white wines like Pouilly-Fuissé or reds like Beaujolais.

Côtes de porc à la gasconne [koht duh pohr ah lah gas-kawn]
Marinated chops are browned lightly, then baked with garlic and olives, and served with the stock, which has been reduced with white wine. Serve with white Graves or red St. Émilion.

Costoletta alla milanese [kos-to-*leht*-tah *ah*-lah mee-lah-*neh*-zeh]
The ubiquitous breaded veal cutlet sautéed in butter, although much more interesting ways of serving are *alla bolognese*, simmered in tomato sauce to which cheese, ham, and truffles have been added, or *a scottadito* (skawt-tah-*dee*-to), rubbed with oil, salt, and pepper, and broiled over coals. Serve with dry white wines like Orvieto or light reds like Valtellina or Bardolino.

Costoletta alla valdostana [kos-to-*leht*-tah *ah*-lah vahl-do-*sta*-nah]
A breaded veal cutlet that has been slit and stuffed with white truffles, cheese, and ground beef, then fried. Serve with a dry white wine like Cortese or a light red like Freisa.

Couscous [koose-koose]
An ancient North African specialty of any of various steamed grains or legumes—semolina, rice, or chickpeas—with chunks of mutton, pimiento, carrots, turnip, and sometimes cabbage, vegetable marrow, pumpkin or squash. Serve with reds like Beaujolais, or *rosés*.

Croque-monsieur [krohk-muh-suhr]
Small ham and cheese sandwiches sautéed in butter, and excellent with dry white wines or Champagne.

Culotte de bœuf [külot duh buhf]
The rump of beef, also called the flank, aitchbone, or silver-
side, generally braised. This pot roast is usually marinated.
Served with vegetables cooked with it, or a variety of garnishes,
accompanied with hearty red wines like Burgundies or Rhônes.

Daube de bœuf tourangelle [dohb duh buhf too-rahn-zhell]
Originally, a *daube* was braised meat intended to be eaten cold,
but today it is usually beef braised in highly spiced red wine,
often served hot, or warmed-over. The Touraine fashion includes an oxtail with the flank steak, braised in Chinon with
mushrooms and carrots, shallots, onions, and garlic. *Daube des
Charentes* (shah-rahnt) calls additionally for nutmeg, vinegar
and Cognac, and a *bouquet garni* in place of the mushrooms.
Serve with full red wines like Chinon or Beaujolais.

Daurade farcie [do-rahd far-see]
A delicate Mediterranean fish, baked and served with fried
tomatoes, anchovies, and green olives in Nice. Elsewhere, it is
often stuffed with mussels and crab, mashed potatoes and
spinach, onion, garlic and herbs, then baked and served on
fennel. Served with local wines, white or *rosé*.

Dinde aux marrons [dand oh mahr-rohn]
Roast turkey stuffed with the chopped liver, pork, veal, and
chicken, with thyme and nutmeg, brandy and roasted chestnuts.
Serve with full red Côte d'Or Burgundies.

Doratini di ricotta romano [do-rah-*tee*-nee dee ree-*kot*-tah ro-
mah-nah]
These cheese fritters are a particular glorification of Rome's
soft ricotta cheese, made by chilling a mixture of cheese, flour,
and egg, seasoned with grated lemon rind, salt, and brandy,
forming this into balls then frying them until golden. Served
with grillades and mixed fries, or as a dessert when sprinkled
with sugar. Serve with dry white wines like Frascati, or fruity
reds like Chianti.

Écrevisses à la bordelaise   [ay-kreh-vees ah lah bor-duh-layz]
Crayfish, an outstanding French delicacy, first sautéed in butter then simmered with a *mirepoix* of minced onions and carrots, thyme, laurel and parsley, after being moistened with white Graves and flamed in Cognac, the sauce being thickened with yolks and butter; *à la bressane* (bres-san) *en buisson* (on bwee-sawn), and *au court-bouillon* (koor-boo-yawn) call for boiling the crayfish in a white wine bouillon. Accompany with dry whites like Chablis or Muscadet.

Eisbein   [*ice*-bine]
Pickled pigs' knuckles simmered with root vegetables. These shanks are invariably accompanied with sauerkraut that is often cooked with chopped onions and apples; served with boiled potatoes, and beer or Steinwein.

Empanada   [ehm-pah-*nah*-dah]
Meat pies of various combinations are favorite Spanish dishes, usually starting with onions sautéed in olive oil, and tomato or saffron, along with other seasonings. Serve with red or white Rioja.

Entrecôte   [ahn-truh-kawt]
The sirloin steak, cut from the short loin, usually grilled, and served with any of dozens of sauces and garnishes, and accompanied with fruity wines like Beaujolais or Rhônes.

Entrecôte a l'échalote   [on-truh-kawt ah lay-shah-lot]
This Burgundian way of sautéing a rib steak, then adding red wine, shallots, and mushroom to the pan juices, is a perfect foil for hearty red Burgundies: *à la bordelaise* calls for serving the charcoal-broiled steak with *sauce bordelaise* and water cress, which tastes fine with a Médoc or St. Émilion.

Épaule de mouton   [ay-pol duh moo-tawn]
Mutton shoulder, usually boned and rolled, sometimes in the shape of a ball, stuffed and then braised or roasted, in the ways used for leg of lamb or mutton. Serve with hearty reds like Rhônes.

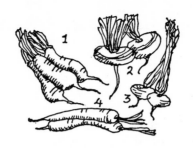

Escargots à la bourguignonne [ess-kar-go ah lah boor-gheen-yawn]
Piping hot snails that have been boiled in a white wine bouillon, put back in the shells with Burgundy butter—which includes minced garlic, shallots and parsley—sprinkled with
bread crumbs, and finished in a hot oven; *de Chablis* omits the
shallots; *à la bordelaise* adds ham; *aux noix* (oh nwah) calls
for serving the snails in a sauce to which ham browned in olive
oil, and mashed walnuts, are added. Accompany with full white
Burgundies or reds like Beaujolais.

Estofado Rosalia [es-to-*fah*-doh ro-sa-*lee*-yah]
Beef slices stewed with ham and seasonings, in beef stock,
served sprinkled with parsley. Serve with red Rioja.

Estouffat [es-toof-fah]
Flank steak braised for a day in red wine—also with Armagnac
in Gascony—with bones, vegetables, and spices, so that the re-
sulting *daube* (dohb) is well concentrated. Serve with hearty
reds like Rhônes or St. Émilion.

Fagiano alla panna [fah-*jah*-no ahl-la *pahn*-nah]
Pheasant sautéed in butter in a casserole, then stewed with
cream and lemon juice; *in casseruola* (een kahs-sehr-*woh*-la),
the pheasant is sautéed in butter, then white wine, Muscat
grapes and Marsala or Madeira are added for the stewing, the
bird being flamed in brandy before serving. *Farcito* (far-*chee*-
to) is done much the same way, first stuffing the pheasant with
chopped veal, onions, and truffles, adding bread crumbs and
herbs, then moistening with white wine, and stewing the bird
in more white wine; *con verdura* (vair-*doo*-rah) is the same

casserole preparation, but onions, mushrooms, and Marsala are added. Serve with any full white wine like Orvieto, or a full red wine like Barolo.

Faisan à la choucroute   [fay-zahn ah la shoo-kroot]
Braised pheasant with sauerkraut and sausages. Serve with flowery white Traminer or beer.

Faux filet   [foh fee-lay]
The loin of beef, same as *contrefilet*, usually grilled as steaks, served with a variety of garnishes, and accompanied with red wines like Burgundies.

Fegato alla veneziana   [*feh*-gah-toh *ahl*-lah veh-neh-*tsyah*-nah]
The original calf's liver and onions, thin slices sautéed in oil and butter with plenty of onions, parsley, and pepper; *alla romana* is spitted chunks of pig's liver—*fegatelli di maiale* (*feh*-gah-*tehl*-lee dee mah-*yah*-leh)—alternating with ham, garlic bread, and bay leaves, roasted over coals; *alla fiorentina* is the same way, except the pig's liver is coated with bread crumbs mixed with chopped fennel, parsley, and garlic, the ham being omitted; *all'italiana* is thin slices stewed in a casserole, with layers of a filling of chopped mushrooms and parsley, onion and garlic, seasoned with bay, basil, and thyme, served with a sauce made by adding butter, lemon, and vinegar to the pan juices. Serve with any full white wine, like Orvieto, or a light red like Bardolino.

Fettuccine alla romana   [feht-too-*chee*-neh *ahl*-lah roh-*mah*-nah]
The most succulent and famous of all Roman *pasta* dishes, thin egg noodles less than half an inch wide are brought piping hot to your table, a great chunk of butter is swirled into the golden coils, along with sprinkled clouds of Parmigiano or Romano, and then a glistening mound is piled on your plate. Serve with a dry white like Frascati or a light red like Chianti.

Filet de bœuf   [fee-lay duh buhf]
The tenderloin, or undercut of the loin, which is generally roasted when cooked whole, can be served with dozens of

garnishes, and accompanied with full-bodied reds such as Côte d'Or Burgundies.

Filet mignon   [fee-lay meen-yawn]
The tenderest of steaks, from the short end of the tenderloin, usually grilled, often after being dipped in butter and bread crumbs, and served with a variety of sauces and garnishes. Often served with delicate red Burgundies from the Côte d'Or or Bordeaux reds from the Médoc and Graves.

Foie gras   [fwah grah]
Fat livers are obtained by forced feeding of geese, the best coming from Alsace and Gascony; *pâté de foie gras* is a paste made from such livers, usually with truffles, and not so good as the livers by themselves. They are occasionally sautéed, braised with white wine, and made into terrines, but they are best by themselves, spread on crisp breads and accompanied with Champagne or a fine red wine of Burgundy or Bordeaux.

Fondant   [fohn-dahn]
A purée, usually chicken or wild fowl, mixed with a reduced sauce or second purée, usually ham or liver, chilled, formed into croquettes, dipped in thickened egg and bread crumbs, then quickly deep-fried and served with fried parsley and dry white wines like Pouilly-Fuissé, *rosé* wines like Tavel, or fruity red wines like Beaujolais: *à la Bohème* (bo-ehm), of ham, foie gras and cream sauce; *à la comtesse* (kohn-tes), of chicken and tongue; *à la duchesse*, of chicken, tongue, and pistachio nuts; *à la reine*, of chicken and *sauce suprème; à la Marion*, of chicken and game.

Fond blanc   [fohn blahn]
White stock made from veal bones, a base for sauces.

Fond brun   [fohn bran]
Brown stock made from beef and veal bones, a sauce base.

Fond de poisson   [fohn duh pwah-son]
White stock from fish, a base for sauces.

Fond de volaille [fohn duh vo-ly-yuh]
White stock from fowl and veal bones, a base for sauces.

Fondue à la Fendant [fohn-dü ah lah fon-dahn]
This gustatory game of the Swiss is now universal, and while traditionally made with the white wine of Fendant, Neuchâtel is frequently used. A chafing dish is rubbed with garlic, half filled with wine in which Gruyère or Emmenthaler is melted, then spiced with white pepper, cayenne and Kirsch, thickened with arrowroot or potato flour, and kept hot during the serving. Pieces of bread are speared with a fork and dipped into the melted cheese. If the bread falls in the dish, the forfeit is to drink your glass of Fendant. Serve with a green salad and the same Swiss wine used for the *fondue*.

Fonduta [fohn-*doo*-ta]
A glorious Italian version of the Swiss fondue, made with Fontina cheese and eggs, with white truffles. Serve with any Piedmont wine.

Fricandeau [free-kahn-do]
Braised or pan-fried slices of veal loin, generally served with light reds like Beaujolais or Graves.

Fricassée alsacienne [free-kah-say al-sas-yen]
Browned chicken stewed in white wine with mushrooms; *la fricassée de Caion* (kah-yawn) is marinated pork loin browned in butter and fat, then stewed in red wine and the marinade, the sauce thickened with cream and blood. Accompany with a light red like Beaujolais.

Frittata alla Ciriacese [freet-*tah*-tah *ahl*-lah chee-ree-ah-*cheh*-zeh]
An omelet of anchovies and tuna fish, spiced with nutmeg, garlic, pepper, and parsley. Serve with a white wine like Orvieto.

Fritto misto [*free*-toh *mees*-toh]
The glorious mixed fry of Italy—sautéed in butter in Milan and in oil in Florence—pieces of lamb, chicken livers, brains, sweetbreads, artichokes, marrows, and so forth, breaded and

served with slices of lemon. The Genoese version is magnificently made with fish. Serve with dry white Orvieto, light red Chianti, or any local dry wine.

Friture [free-tür]
A mixed fry, of small breaded fish on the Loire, of larger fish on the Rhône, and in Périgord and Quercy, where walnut oil is used and garlic and parsley are added. Related to the *matelote*, which is a stew. Serve with dry white wines like Muscadet.

Galimafrée [gah-lee-mah-fray]
A ham stew, or one with hashed lamb or chicken, with plenty of onions and other vegetables, done in stock, then browned in the oven. Serve with red wines like Beaujolais.

Gallina en pepitoria [gahl-*yee*-nah en peh-pee-*tor*-yah]
A classic Spanish chicken fricassee, lightly sautéed pieces of chicken—or just giblets—being coated in a batter, then lightly sautéed and stewed in dry Sherry with chopped onion, parsley, and laurel, finished with mashed almonds, garlic, and hard-boiled egg yolks that have been moistened with broth, then added to the fricassee in the last minutes of cooking. Guadalajara specialty. Serve with an old red Rioja or a dry white Rioja.

Garbure [gar-bür]
A thick and aromatic soup, almost a stew, mostly of herbs, green vegetables, and meat, like the Spanish *cocida* (ko-*thee*-dah). Serve with beer or Beaujolais.

Africaine [ah-free-kehn]
Dishes that contain ingredients from Africa, such as eggplant, curries, pistachio or other nuts, bananas, and so on, including some that were inspired by the Meyerbeer opera. The garnish for roasts is mushrooms, cucumbers and eggplant sautéed in oil; the grilled sole is with sliced bananas in lemon juice, with a *sauce diable*; the grilled tournedos is served with fried bananas. Tomatoes and castle potatoes are usually included.

Agnès Sorel [ahn-yehs so-rel]
Dishes served with tarts filled with minced tongue, mushroom and truffle, with a sauce made from the stock and blended with Madeira and *demi-glace*.

Albufèra [ahl-bü-fay-rah]
Poached poultry dishes served with tartlets filled with mushroom caps, tiny chicken dumplings, and chopped kidneys, decorated with truffle and tongue, bound with *sauce albufèra*.

Alexandra
Dishes named after Edward VII's queen, with sliced truffles and artichoke hearts or asparagus tips, and often a Madeira or cream sauce, as well.

Algérienne [ahl-zheh-ree-an]
Dishes garnished with potato croquettes and small braised tomatoes, plus a tomato sauce occasionally.

Allemande [al-mahnd]
Dishes originating in Germany, particularly stewed or braised meats; those garnished with sauerkraut, salt pork, smoked sausages, and noodles or mashed potatoes; or those served with a sauce made of veal stock, cream and yolks, with lemon juice and nutmeg.

Alsacienne [al-sas-yen]
Dishes served with sauerkraut, and often ham, sausages, and potatoes. A traditional meat garnish is braised cabbage, Fondante potatoes (blanched and cooked in butter), and the

Garnishes (continued)

brown sauce, *demi-glace,* or sautéed noodles with diced truffles and foie gras.

Ambassadeur [ahm-bahs-sah-duhr]

For large cuts, Duchess potatoes, artichoke bottoms with a purée of mushrooms, and horseradish.

Ambassadrice [ahm-bahs-sah-drees]

Small pieces of meat or fowl are garnished with sautéed mushrooms and chicken livers, cockscombs and truffles, or sweetbreads and asparagus, all with a Madeira sauce.

Américaine [ah-may-rih-kehn]

The French idea of the American way, various fish and sea foods served with creamed tomato sauce that contains lobster meat and coral; or garnished with lobster tail slices and truffles.

Ancienne [ahn-syen]

Most simply, a garnish of mushroom caps and braised onions for fowl, fish, and sea food; but truffles, chicken dumplings, and crayfish cooked in bouillon are often the garnish for delicate dishes like calf's brains, poached fowl, and *vol-au-vents.*

Andalouse [ahn-dah-looz]

The southern Spanish province names dishes made or garnished with peppers, particularly pimiento or capsicum, tomatoes and olives, or eggplant, and *chipolata* (chee-poh-*lah*-tah) sausages.

Anglaise [ahn-glehz]

Garnish of boiled vegetables or those cooked with the meat or fowl, mostly turnips, carrots, cauliflower, potatoes.

Anna

The French chef Dugléré devised this way of doing potatoes, which are thinly sliced, placed in layers in a covered pan, dotted with butter, then baked in the oven. A favorite meat garnish.

Anversoise [ahn-vair-swahz]

A meat garnish of creamed hop shoots, and boiled potatoes.

Garnishes (continued)

Archiduc [ahr-shih-dük]
Name for dishes seasoned with paprika and cream.

Ardennaise [ahr-den-nehz]
Name for fowl dishes prepared in casserole, with juniper.

Argenteuil [ahr-zhahn-teu-yuh]
A region famous for its asparagus that names many dishes so garnished.

Arlequin [arl-kan]
Name used primarily for party dishes of many colors.

Arlésienne [ahr-lehz-yen]
Various garnishes for meats, mainly fried eggplant, or onion rings, and sautéed or stuffed tomatoes.

Armenonville [ahr-muh-nawn-veel]
A meat garnish named after the Parisian restaurant that made it famous, composed of potatoes Anna, creamed morels, and tarts filled with diced cockscomb and kidney; or buttered artichoke hearts, tomatoes, potatoes, and string beans.

Artagnan [ar-tahn-yawn]
Garnish for meat and fowl, named after the musketeer, composed of mushrooms in *sauce béarnaise*, small stuffed tomatoes, and potato croquettes.

Artois [ahr-twah]
This province lends its name to dishes that incorporate light puff pastry.

Athénienne [ah-tehn-yen]
Dishes named after the Greek city are generally seasoned with onions and garnished with eggplant, tomatoes, and pimiento.

Aurore [oh-roar]
Fowl and fish dishes, particularly, that are given a rosy color and piled high on the plate, usually served with *sauce Aurore.*

Autrichienne [oh-treesh-yen]
Name for many dishes seasoned with paprika or sour cream.

Garnishes (continued)

Badoise [bah-dwahz]
Braised red cabbage, bacon and mashed potatoes; or pitted cherries for small cuts.

Banquière [bahn-kyehr]
Garnish for poached or braised fowl or brains, and *vol-au-vents*, consisting of chicken dumplings, mushrooms, and sliced truffles, or stuffed larks, with *sauce banquière*.

Baron Brisse [ba-rohn brees]
A garnish for grilled or sautéed steaks; tomatoes, chopped and then sautéed, are placed on the steak, which is garnished with potatoes soufflé and artichoke bottoms filled with truffle balls, all with a *demi-glace*.

Batelière [bah-tel-yare]
Fish garnish of mushrooms, glazed onions, crayfish and fried eggs.

Bayonnaise [bah-yaw-nehz]
Bayonne, a city of the Pyrennees famous for its ham, names many dishes so garnished.

Béatrix [bay-ah-treex]
Meat garnish of sautéed new potatoes and morels, glazed new carrots, and braised artichoke hearts.

Beauharnais [bo-ar-nay]
Garnish for tournedos and noisettes: small sautéed potatoes, stuffed mushrooms and artichoke hearts, with *béarnaise sauce* blended with tarragon purée.

Garnishes (continued)

Belle-Hélène [bell-eh-lehn]
For large cuts, grilled mushrooms filled with tomato, potato croquettes, new peas and carrots.

Berrichonne [bair-ree-shawn]
For large cuts, whole onions and chestnuts, braised cabbage balls, and bacon.

Bohémienne [bo-ehm-yen]
Rice pilaf, sautéed tomatoes, fried onion rings; or tartlets filled with chopped foie gras and truffles.

Bonne-femme [bon-fam]
Garnish cooked with the fowl, consisting of small potatoes and onions, with bacon, and minced onions.

Bordelaise [bor-duh-layz]
Garnish for meats: sautéed potatoes and cêpes. Fowl garnish; braised artichoke hearts, sautéed diced potatoes, fried parsley and onion rings. Or with red wine *sauce bordelaise*.

Boulangère [boo-lahn-zhair]
Garnish of quartered potatoes and onions cooked with the joint or roast.

Bouquetière [boo-kuh-tyair]
Garnish of a variety of buttered vegetables, covered with hollandaise or the meat juices, arranged around the roast.

Bourgeoise [boor-zhwahz]
For braised meats: glazed onions and carrots, with bacon.

Bourguignonne [boor-gheen-yawn]
Garnish for large pieces of beef; browned onions, sautéed mushrooms, diced bacon. Usually with *sauce bourguignonne*.

Brabançonne [brah-bahn-son]
Garnish for large pieces of meat: braised endives and fondant potatoes; also tarts filled with Brussels sprouts and covered with Mornay sauce, and thin potato croquettes.

Bragance [brah-gahns]
Garnish for tournedos and noisettes: small tomatoes filled with *sauce béarnaise*, and potato croquettes; or puff-paste tartlets filled with asparagus tips, with truffle sauce.

Garnishes (continued)

Bretonne [bruh-ton]

Garnish for roasts: white kidney beans in Breton sauce, with chopped parsley. Breton sauce is used for fish.

Brillat-Savarin [bree-yah sah-vah-ran]

Garnish for wild fowl and meat: tarts filled with minced *foie gras* and truffles, bound with *demi-glace*.

Bruxelloise [brü-sell-wahz]

Garnish for meats: steamed Brussels sprouts and braised endive, with potatoes sautéed in butter.

Camerani [cah-may-rah-nee]

Garnish for poultry and sweetbreads: tarts filled with *foie gras* purée, slices of truffle and tongue, with macaroni, in a supreme sauce.

Canova [kah-*noh*-va]

A garnish for steaks and poultry of sautéed *foie gras* slices, along with truffles, cockscomb, and kidneys that are often chopped and put in artichoke bottoms, the whole served with *sauce madère*.

Cardinal

Name given to fish and sea-food dishes that are brightened with red, especially lobster coral.

Carignan [kah-reen-yahn]

A meat garnish composed of a base of potatoes Anna, and asparagus tips.

Castiglione [kah-stee-*lyoh*-neh]

Meat garnish of large mushrooms filled with rice, ham, and cheese, with sautéed eggplant, and poached marrow slices.

Catalane [kah-tah-lahn]

Garnish for meats: sauté of diced eggplant, with rice pilaf, plus a tomato sauce; or artichoke hearts and grilled tomatoes.

Châlonnaise [shah-lawn-nehz]

Garnish for fowl, sweetbreads, and white braises: tarts with cockscomb and truffle slices, with *sauce suprême*.

Chambord [shahm-bord]

Garnish for large fish: fish dumplings decorated with truffles, filets of sole, sautéed roe, poached crayfish, truffles, mushrooms, and fried croutons, with red wine sauce.

Chanoinesse [shah-nwah-ness]
This cannoness's garnish is creamed carrots with truffles in patty shells, served with a Sherry sauce, to accompany sweetbreads, poached eggs, or chicken breasts.

Chantilly [shahn-tee-yee]
District famous for cream and peas; the name is used for dishes served with whipped cream.

Charollaise [shah-rol-lehz]
Tartlets filled with turnip purée, and cauliflower.

Chasseur [shah-suhr]
Dishes served hunter's style are garnished with chopped mushrooms that have been sautéed with shallots and white wine, or with *sauce chasseur*.

Chartres [shar-truh]
Stuffed mushrooms and lettuce; or glazed turnips and purées of peas and potatoes; or fondant potatoes with blanched tarragon.

Château [shah-toe]
Primarily the name given to quartered potatoes that have been lightly sautéed in butter, then roasted, but the name is sometimes given to roasts garnished with these "castle" potatoes.

Châtelaine [shat-lehn]
This "queen of the castle" garnish for meat and poultry is artichoke bottoms filled with chestnut purée, or vegetables plus braised celery and sautéed potatoes, with a sauce made from the stock.

Chevreuse [sheh-vruhz]
Steak garnish of chopped or puréed mushrooms on artichoke bottoms or croquettes, and a slice of truffle on the steak.

Chinonaise [she-no-naze]
Garnish for meats: braised cabbage balls stuffed with sausage meat, and parsley potatoes, with *demi-glace*.

Garnishes (continued)

Chipolata [she-po-lah-tah]
Garnish for meat and fowl: braised chestnuts, glazed onions, mushrooms, small pork sausages, diced bacon, accompanied by a sauce from the stock or *demi-glace*.

Choisy [shwah-zee]
Steak garnish, the cut being placed on toast and served with braised hearts of lettuce and *château* potatoes, with a meat glaze or brown sauce.

Choron [sho-rawn]
Garnish for grilled or sautéed tournedos and noisettes: artichoke bottoms filled with green peas or asparagus tips, and sautéed potatoes, along with a *sauce béarnaise* containing tomato.

Clamart [klah-mar]
Meat garnish like Choron, but with purée of peas, and a rich *demi-glace*.

Claremont
Meat garnish of stuffed onions, braised cucumbers and chopped tomatoes, with *demi-glace*.

Clermont [klare-mawn]
Meat garnish of braised stuffed cabbage balls and salt pork, with sautéed potatoes and *demi-glace*. A variation is a mold of poached, creamed chestnuts, with fried onion rings.

Colbert [kohl-bair]
A steak garnish, the steak being placed on a chicken croquette, covered with *sauce madère*, after which a fried egg and a slice of truffle is placed on top.

Garnishes (continued)

Concorde
Peas, potato purée, glazed carrots.

Condé [con-deh]
With a purée of red beans.

Conti [kohn-tee]
Meat garnish: balls of lentil purée with rissolé potatoes, and, sometimes, diced bacon, served with *demi-glace*.

Crécy [kray-see]
Various dishes that contain carrots, usually creamed or puréed. The steak garnish is sliced carrots in *sauce madère*, the fowl garnish and omelet filling are creamed carrots julienne.

Cussy [kü-see]
Garnish for meat and fowl: artichoke bottoms stuffed with mushroom or chestnut purée and baked with a sprinkle of cheese, cockscombs, and truffles cooked in Madeira, with Port or Madeira sauce.

Daumet or **Daumont** [do-meh, do-mawn]
Garnish for braised fish: mushrooms or tarts filled with crayfish tails in *sauce Nantua*, truffled fish dumplings, filets of sole or roe that have been deep fried, the whole served with Norman sauce or crayfish butter.

Dauphine [do-feen]
Meat garnish of Dauphine potatoes, which are riced and mixed with cream-puff paste, then formed into balls and deep fried.

Dauphinoise [do-feen-wahz]
Dishes that have been sprinkled with grated Swiss cheese, then dotted with butter, and browned.

Dieppoise [dyep-pwahz]
Name for dishes of salt-water fish that have been poached in white wine, then garnished with mussels and shrimp, the sauce being made from the stock and more white wine.

Doria [doe-ree-ah]
Name for dishes that are garnished with cucumber balls sautéed in butter, with garlic.

Garnishes (continued)

Du Barry [dü bah-ree]
The name of Louis XV's favorite usually indicates cauliflower in a dish. As a meat garnish, baked buds in a white or brown sauce and sprinkled with cheese are often used.

Duchesse [dü-shes]
Meat garnish of Duchess potatoes, which are mashed, mixed with yolks and butter, then formed into balls, or borders around the meat, and browned in the oven. They are also dipped in yolk, then crumbs, and fried.

Duroc [dü-rawk]
Garnish for meat and fowl of new potatoes rissolé, or browned quickly in butter, usually served with *sauce chausseur*.

Duse [dü-zuh]
Meat garnish of French beans, peeled tomatoes and diced potatoes, sautéed in butter.

Duxelles [dü-sel]
Garnish for meats, chopped mushrooms sautéed in butter and oil, mixed with chopped onions and shallots moistened with white wine, and chopped parsley added.

Excelsior
Fondant potatoes and braised lettuce.

Favart [fah-var]
Garnish for fowl or sweetbreads: chicken dumplings with chopped tarragon, and pastry tarts filled with sautéed mushrooms mixed with cream.

Fermière [fehrm-yair]
A garnish for braised and sautéed meats, consisting of sliced carrot, turnip, and chopped celery root, first sautéed in butter, then reduced in stock.

Financière [fee-nahn-syair]
Garnish for meat and fowl of button mushrooms, truffle slices, cockscombs, chicken dumplings, and sometimes blanched olives and crayfish.

Garnishes (continued)

Flamande [flah-mahnd]
Garnish for meats of braised stuffed cabbage balls, glazed carrots and turnips, potatoes and sausage.

Fleuriste [fleu-reest]
Garnish for steaks cooked in butter and covered with a *demi-glace*, consisting of scooped-out tomatoes filled with a dice of fresh vegetables.

Florentine
French dishes cooked in the Florentine manner usually call for a bed of spinach, usually puréed, the whole coated with *sauce Mornay*, sprinkled with grated cheese, then glazed.

Fondant [fon-dahn]
Like castle potatoes, cooked in butter and covered, often moistened with consommé.

Forestière [for-es-tyair]
Meat or fowl garnish of sautéed morels or other mushrooms, and buttered potatoes.

Française [frahn-sehz]
Meat garnish of fried mashed potato patties filled with finely diced vegetables, along with asparagus tips, braised lettuce, and cauliflower buds in hollandaise; or just leaf spinach and potatoes Anna.

Frascati [frah-*skah*-tee]
Meat garnish of large baked mushrooms, some filled with asparagus tips, others with diced truffle, along with sautéed slices of *foie gras*, with Port sauce.

Gastronome
Garnish for fowl, sweetbreads and steaks of glazed chestnuts, truffles, and cocks' kidneys, with *demi-glace*.

Gauloise [gohl-wahz]
Garnish for meat and fowl of tarts filled with cocks' kidneys, and mushrooms, truffle slices, cockscombs Villeroi, with a sauce made by adding white wine to the meat stock.

Génoise [zhen-wahz]
A cold mayonnaise blended with mashed pistachios, almonds,

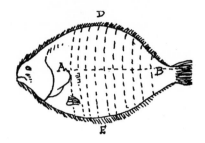

Garnishes (continued)

and herbs; a brown fish sauce made of stock, red wine, anchovies, and butter; or the classic spongecake—all named after Genoa, where they were supposed to have originated, and all classics of French cuisine.

Genovese [jeh-no-veh-zeh]

Generally, a dish flavored with *il pesto,* the famous Genoese sauce for soups and *pasta* that contains chopped basil, pine nuts, and garlic mixed with oil and cheese.

Godard [go-dar]

Garnish for meat and fowl: large and small dumplings, with cockscombs and kidneys, whole truffles, and sweetbreads, served with Godard sauce.

Gorenflot [go-ren-flo]

Garnish for joints, red cabbage and sausage braised together, with boiled potatoes.

Grand duc [grahn dük]

A garnish that invariably includes asparagus and sliced truffles; with prawns and *sauce Mornay* for fish; with *demi-glace* for fowl; and with the same sauce and blanched beef marrow for steaks sautéed in butter.

Grecque [grek]

Garnish of pilaf or timbale of rice with sautéed onions, served with a tomato sauce, decorated with diced pimiento.

Henri IV [on-ree katr]

Garnish for tournedos and noisettes: artichoke bottoms filled with *sauce béarnaise* mixed with veal glaze, and braised potatoes, served with a Madeira sauce. Also, poached eggs on grilled ham, with *béarnaise,* or fried potatoes and water cress.

Garnishes (continued)

Hongroise [awn-grwahz]
With paprika and cream. Garnish for meat: cauliflower buds in Mornay sauce with paprika, fondant potatoes; sometimes, rice pilaf, particularly with fowl.

Hôtelière [oht-lyair]
Fish or steaks served with herb butter, or maître d'hotel sauce, and sautéed mushrooms.

Hussarde [üs-sard]
"Cavalier" fashion generally means horseradish in a dish. The meat garnish is potatoes and mushrooms or eggplant stuffed with puréed onion, with grated horseradish. The egg dish is fried bread spread with chopped ham and onions or mushrooms, crowned by a slice of fried tomato and a poached egg, with hollandaise or a *velouté* with cayenne.

Impériale [am-pair-yahl]
Various ornate garnishes that include truffles, *foie gras*, cockscombs and kidneys, with sauces.

Indienne [an-dyen]
Various dishes, particularly fish and fowl, that are garnished with curried rice or a curried sauce.

Italienne [ee-tahl-yen]
Dishes of the French cuisine that are served with diced mushroom, or tomato sauce, or *pasta*.

Jardinière [zhar-deen-yair]
Meat garnish of spring vegetables, often diced.

Jessica
Garnish for poached eggs, fowl or veal: small artichoke bottoms stuffed with marrow and shallots, sautéed morels, and molded potatoes Anna, all with thickened *sauce allemande*.

Joinville [zhwan-veel]
Garnish for fish of shrimp and crayfish, truffles, and mushrooms, in a thickened white or Norman sauce.

Judic [zhü-deek]
Dishes that are bedded on shredded lettuce, or call for braised lettuce as a garnish, stuffed with ham or served with cockscombs and kidneys.

Garnishes (continued)

Languedocienne [lahng-doh-syen]
Garnish for meat and fowl: mushrooms and tomatoes, sautéed, fried eggplant, with a tomatoed *demi-glace* sauce.

Liègeoise [lee-ehzh-wahz]
Game birds and kidneys prepared with juniper berries.

Lorette
Chicken croquettes, truffle slices, asparagus tips.

Lorraine [lor-rehn]
Dishes with bacon and Gruyère cheese, or a garnish for braised meats of red cabbage braised in red wine, and *fondant* (fohn-dahn) potatoes, with horseradish in the sauce.

Lyonnaise [lee-ohn-nehz]
Dishes with sautéed onions, particularly a meat garnish of fried onions, with brown gravy. Also, hashed browned potatoes.

Macédoine [mah-say-dwahn]
Meat garnish: diced vegetables cooked in butter; often green peas and beans in cream sauce with cauliflower buds.

Maillot [my-yoh]
Garnish for ham and meats: Glazed carrots and turnips, string beans sautéed in butter, and braised lettuce sometimes accompanied with buttered onions and cauliflower buds, served with Madeira sauce.

Marchand de vin [mar-shahn duh van]
Dishes in the "wine merchant's" style are fish and steaks served with a red wine sauce, and are accompanied with fruity red wines like Beaujolais.

Maréchale [mah-reh-shahl]
Thin cuts of meat and fish filets that are breaded and sautéed, generally served with asparagus and truffles, accompanied with fresh young reds like Beaujolais or dry whites like Muscadet.

Marengo [mah-rehng-go]
A dish originally improvised on the battlefield for Napoleon by Dunand, and now chicken or veal sautéed with garlic and tomatoes in oil, garnished with a fried egg, and crayfish.

Garnishes (continued)

Marigny [mah-reen-yee]

Meat garnish or tartlets filled alternately with peas and string beans, and *fondant* potatoes, often with Madeira sauce.

Mascotte [mahs-kot]

Garnish for meat and fowl cooked *en cocotte:* quartered sautéed artichoke hearts and tiny potatoes browned in butter, with truffle slices or balls, and white wine sauce from the stock.

Masséna [mahs-say-nah]

Garnish for small cuts of meat, fowl, and poached eggs: artichoke bottoms filled with *sauce Périgueux* and poached slices of marrow.

Matelote [mat-lot]

Fish garnish of sautéed mushrooms and glazed onions, croutons fried in butter, and crayfish, served with *matelote sauce.*

Melba

Garnish for small meat cuts: small tomatoes stuffed with diced chicken, braised lettuce, and truffles and mushrooms blended with *velouté* and cheese, with Port sauce.

Mentonnaise [mahn-tawn-nehz]

Meat garnish of small braised artichokes, slices of vegetable marrow or squash stuffed with rice and tomato, or stuffed chard, and riced potatoes. Also, dishes prepared with tomatoes, black olives, and garlic.

Meunière [muhn-yair]

Fish sautéed in the fashion of the "miller's wife," now one of the simplest and best ways of preparing fish, which is first lightly floured and seasoned, then after cooking the pan butter is poured over, and the fish is sprinkled with lemon and chopped parsley. Accompany such fish with white wines like Muscadet or Graves.

Mikado

Garnish for small meat cuts of curried rice and grilled tomatoes.

Milanaise [mee-lah-nehz]

Meat garnish of macaroni or *gnocchi* with tomato sauce.

Garnishes (continued)

Mirabeau [mee-rah-bo]
Garnish for grilled meats of pitted olives, anchovies, and blanched tarragon leaves, served with water cress and anchovy butter.

Moderne
Garnish for large meat cuts of diced, jellied vegetables in small molds, stuffed braised lettuce, and veal dumplings decorated with tongue, served with Madeira sauce; or cauliflower in cheese sauce, stuffed tomatoes, and Duchess potatoes.

Montmorency [mawn-mor-on-see]
The most famous cherries of France, from the district near Enghien, and thus the name for dishes including them; or buttered artichoke bottoms, carrots and potatoes.

Montpensier [mawn-pon-syeh]
For small cuts: artichoke hearts, buttered asparagus and potatoes, truffle slices, often with Madeira sauce.

Nantaise [non-tehz]
Glazed turnips, peas, and potato purée.

Nantua [nahn-chwah]
Name given to dishes that are garnished with crayfish.

Niçoise [nee-swahz]
Name for dishes prepared mainly with tomatoes and garlic.

Ninon [nee-nohn]
Garnish for small meat cuts of mashed potato molds filled with cockscombs and kidneys in a *velouté* sauce, and buttered asparagus with sauce containing marrow.

Garnishes (continued)

Nivernaise [nee-vehr-naze]
Meat garnish of glazed carrots, turnips, onions and braised lettuce, boiled potatoes.

Normande [nor-mahnd]
Fish garnish of poached oysters, mussels, crayfish, and shrimp, with mushrooms and truffles, breaded smelt or gudgeon, and croutons fried in butter, served with Norman sauce.

Orientale [or-yahn-tal]
Garnish for meats of rice pilaf cones or tomatoes stuffed with saffron rice, served with tomato sauce.

Orly [or-lee]
A method of cooking fish, dipped in batter and fried in deep fat, served with tomato sauce on the side.

Parisienne [pah-ree-zyehn]
Garnish for meat and fowl of Parisian potatoes—small balls browned in butter then rolled in meat glaze—and braised lettuce, or quartered or stuffed artichokes containing tongue.

Parmentier [par-mahn-tyeh]
The man who brought the potato to France, whose name is used for dishes that include potatoes in their preparation. Particularly, a garnish of cubed potatoes, blanched, then braised in butter.

Paysanne [peh-eezahn]
This "farmer's" garnish from the peasant cookery is braised root vegetables and salt pork, to be served with braised meats and fowl. Celery, onions, lettuce or cabbage, are often included.

Périgourdine [pay-ree-goor-deen]
The district of the best truffles, whose capital is Périgueux, hence dishes garnished with or including truffles, and, often, *foie gras*.

Petit duc [puh-tee dük]
Meat garnish of tarts filled with chicken purée, with truffle slices and asparagus tips. Named after Napoleon's son, whose other title, l'Aiglon, names a similar garnish.

Garnishes (continued)

Portugaise [por-tü-gehz]
Meat·garnish of stuffed tomatoes and *château* potatoes, but, more commonly, chopped meat or forcemeat as a bed or cover for eggs, vegetables, fish.

Princesse [pran-sess]
Garnish for chicken and sweetbreads of diced truffles and asparagus tips, in artichoke bottoms, with *sauce allemande*.

Provençale [pro-von-sahl]
Dishes prepared in olive oil, flavored with garlic and tomato.

Rachel [rah-shell]
Small pieces of grilled meats set on artichoke slices, with poached marrow slices on top, and chopped parsley.

Régence [ray-zhahns]
Garnish for white meats, fowl, sweetbreads, *vol-au-vents*: large and small chicken or veal dumplings, sautéed slices of *foie gras*, cockscombs, mushrooms, and truffles, with a *sauce allemande*. For fish, poached roe and oysters, dumplings.

Renaissance
Garnish for large meat cuts: fresh vegetables placed in groups around the meat, cooked in various simple ways—glazed, braised, rissolé—and including cauliflower buds with hollandaise.

Richelieu [reesh-lyeu]
Garnish for large meat cuts: stuffed tomatoes and mushrooms browned with cheese, braised lettuce, and rissolé potatoes, all with thick veal sauce.

Romaine
Garnish for large meat cuts: small molds of spinach and anchovy, and molds of potatoes Anna, all with a clear tomato sauce. Gnocchi often replaces the potato.

Romanov [ro-mah-nuf]
Meat garnish of cucumbers stuffed with *duxelles* and browned with cheese, and potato tarts filled with diced celery knob and mushrooms bound with *velouté* and sprinkled with horseradish, the whole served with *demi-glace* or Madeira sauce.

Garnishes (continued)

Rossini [rohs-*see*-nee]
Garnish for small meat cuts: thick slices of sautéed *foie gras* and truffle, the whole with Madeira sauce.

Royale [rwhy-al]
Generally, poached fowl in a *sauce velouté* that has been reduced with cream and truffle purée, served hot or cold with a variety of garnishes; or like *Régence*. A light red like Médoc is usually served.

Sagan [sah-gahn]
Garnish for veal scallops, sweetbreads, poached chicken: risotto on which are placed mushrooms stuffed with purée of calf's brains mixed with diced truffles, the whole served with Madeira sauce.

Saint-Germain [san-zhair-man]
Garnish for meats, often called Clarmat, of a purée of green peas, sometimes augmented with artichoke bottoms, glazed carrots, and *sauce béarnaise*.

Sarde [sahrd]
Meat garnish of saffron rice croquettes, sautéed mushrooms, and string beans, or braised and stuffed tomatoes and cucumbers, the whole with a light tomato sauce.

Serge [sairzh]
Garnish for breaded sweetbreads or veal scallops: sautéed quartered artichokes and large julienne of ham warmed in Madeira.

Toulousaine [too-looz-ehn]
Garnish for sweetbreads, *vol-au-vents*, poached fowl: a creamy white stew including cockscombs and kidneys, mushrooms and truffles, chicken dumplings and sweetbreads.

Tourangelle [too-rahn-zhel]
White beans and string beans in a *velouté*.

Trouvillaise [troo-veel-ehz]
Fish garnish of mussels, mushrooms, and shrimps.

Tyrolienne [tee-rol-yen]
Garnish for grillades of fried onion rings, and mashed tomatoes sautéed in butter.

Garnishes (continued)

Valencienne [val-en-syen]
Garnish for small cuts of meat or fowl: rice with pimiento.

Valois [val-wah]
For small meat cuts, a garnish of minced potatoes and slices of artichoke bottoms sautéed *en cocotte*.

Véronique [vay-roh-neek]
Dishes, mostly fish or fowl, prepared with seedless grapes.

Vert-pré [vair-pray]
This garnish of "the green meadows" is water cress with straw potatoes and parsley butter. Also dishes with green vegetables or green sauce.

Vichy
With a purée of carrots.

Victoria
This garnish for small meat cuts is small tomatoes stuffed with mushroom purée and browned with cheese, and quartered artichoke hearts sautéed in butter, the whole served with a Port or Madeira sauce; or macaroni, small tomatoes, braised lettuce, creamed potatoes.

Viennoise [vyen-nwahz]
Garnish for breaded white meats and fowl: hard-boiled yolks and whites chopped separately, anchovies, olives, capers, and lemon slices, all with chopped parsley; or fried noodle nests filled with buttered spinach, celery, potatoes.

Villeroy [veel-rwah]
Way of preparing fowl, fish, and sea food, the raw pieces being dipped in a thickened sauce, then into egg and bread crumbs, and deep-fried. Served with lemon and parsley, or a

Garnishes (continued)

tomato sauce, and various garnishes, generally accompanied with a light white wine like Graves, or a *rosé* like Tavel.

Vladimir [vlah-dee-meer]
Garnish for small meat cuts: pieces of cucumber and squash sautéed in butter.

Walewska [vah-lehf-shka]
A way of preparing fish, particularly sole, the filets being poached in fish stock, set on a platter, garnished with lobster and truffle slices, and coated with *sauce Mornay* that has been reduced with lobster butter. Accompany with a white wine like Graves or Muscadet.

Zingara [zan-gah-rah]
Garnish for meat and fowl composed of thick strips of ham and tongue, mushrooms and truffles, bound with a *demiglace* sauce that has been reduced with tomato and tarragon.

Gasconnade [gas-kawn-nod]
Barbecued leg of mutton stuck with anchovies and garlic, served with a garlic sauce. Accompany with fruity reds like Beaujolais or Rhônes.

Geflügelreis [guh-flü-gul-rys]
Austrian rice mold containing diced boiled chicken and grated Parmesan, which is sprinkled with more cheese and over which tomato sauce is poured. Serve with beer.

Gigot à la ficelle [zhee-go ah lah fee-sel]
Legs of mutton or lamb are usually roasted or braised, but in Bordeaux, the leg is suspended on a cord over a fire of vine branches, the roast finally served with a hot sauce of mashed garlic in vinegar; *gigot à l'eau* is made by putting the leg in water full of herbs and spices, in which it is simmered until the water reduces to a thick gravy, which is finished with butter and vinegar. Serve with St. Émilion or Pomerol.

Gnocchi alla romana [*nyok*-kee *ah*-lah roh-*mah*-nah]
A favorite luncheon dish, small dumplings made of potato

flour or semolina, poached in water or milk, and served with a meat sauce and grated cheese; *alla genovese*, as well as the green gnocchi so popular in Genoa, are served with *il pesto*— the famous basil sauce—or with *tocco* (*tok*-koh), the local meat sauce; *alla piemontese* are potato flour dumplings with those two marks of Piedmont cooking, Parmesan cheese and white truffles, as well as meat sauce. Serve with local wines, either the red Grignolino or Nebbiolo, or white Soave.

Gras-double à la lyonnaise [grah doobl ah la lee-awn-nayz]
The most famous of tripe dishes, the scalded tripe being stewed for hours in bouillon, then braised in fat, sautéed in butter with chopped onions, then sprinkled with parsley. Serve with Beaujolais or red Rhônes.

Gratin dauphinois [gra-tan do-feen-wah]
Gratins are dishes with a crust, often done by sprinkling with bread crumbs and popping the dish into the oven at the last minute; a cheese *gratin* in the Savoy may contain a hash of boiled meat, mushrooms, and macaroni; the Dauphiny version is thinly sliced potatoes with cinnamon and nutmeg, milk, eggs, and cream, topped with grated cheese before baking. Serve with simple grillades or cold meats, and a red wine like Beaujolais.

Grenouilles aux escargots [gruh-noo-yuh ohz es-kar-go]
Sautéed frogs' legs, with snails that have been cooked in white wine then chopped with garlic and shallots, parsley and chives, and sautéed in butter with white wine. This Burgundian specialty is served with Chablis or Meursault.

Grillade marinière [gree-yahd mah-reen-yair]
Layers of flank steak slices and chopped onions, slowly braised and served with a sauce of mashed anchovies, garlic, and parsley simmered in olive oil. Serve with Rhônes.

Grives de vigne [greev duh veen-yuh]
Thrushes wrapped in bacon and roasted over vine cuttings, then served on toast with a sprinkling of olive oil and lemon juice. Serve with red Rhônes or Burgundies.

Guisado de cordero [ghee-*sah*-do deh kor-*deh*-ro]
Lamb stew.

Guisado de trigo [ghee-*sah*-doh deh tree-go]
A sort of ragout or thick wheat porridge, with chickpeas and pig's feet, served with a sauce of tomatoes, red peppers, and onions sautéed in oil, and chopped peppermint. Albacete specialty. Serve with red Rioja.

Hamburger Rauchfleisch [*rowk*-flysh]
Slices of smoked beef brisket, boiled then sliced, served cold with horseradish. Accompany with beer.

Himmel und Erde [*him*-ml oont *ehr*-duh]
"Heaven and earth" is quartered apples and potatoes simmered in water or stock with a bay leaf, then sprinkled with crumbled bacon and served with pork, liver, or sausages, and beer or Rhine wines.

Hochepot [osh-po]
The Flemish version of *pot-au-feu*, which becomes *hutspot* in Holland, must be stirred occasionally while cooking, and contains—at least—breast of beef, mutton shoulder, pig's ears and feet, sausages and potatoes, a variety of root vegetables and herbs, juniper and cloves. Serve with beer or Beaujolais.

Homard à l'américaine [oh-mar ah lah-may-ree-kehn]
Cut-up browned lobster served in a sauce of pounded crabs, tomatoes and shallots, herbs and red pepper, reduced in white wine. Serve with dry whites like Muscadet or Chablis.

Huevos a la flamenca [*hweh*-vohs ah lah flah-*mehn*-kah]
One of the most famous Spanish dishes, "Flemish eggs" are made by sautéing squares of Serrano ham in pork fat with some diced onion, then adding cooked peas, beans, and asparagus tips, followed by diced potatoes, canned pimiento, slices of *chorizo* (choh-*ree*-thoh) (hot pork sausage) and tomato. When these have warmed and mixed together, eggs are broken on this bed, a tablespoon of meat gravy is poured on the raw egg, as well as a strip of pimiento and a sprinkle of parsley, and

then it is put into the oven until the eggs are set. Sevilla specialty. Serve with young red Rioja or Valdepeñas, with a Fino or Manzanilla Sherry or a Montilla, or a dry white Rioja.

Huevos con mariscos [*hweh*-vohs con mah-*ree*-skos]
Eggs beaten and tossed in a frying pan, with mollusks or other shellfish—a sort of scrambled omelet—served with a ring of shrimp, and chopped parsley. Pontevedra specialty, along with *sopa de ostras* (*soh*-pah deh *os*-trahs), oyster soup. Serve with dry or flowery Rioja or Alella.

Huevos escalfados catalana [*hweh*-vohs es-cahl-*fah*-dohs kah-tah-*lah*-nah]
Cold poached eggs on a bed of kidney beans and red peppers, in a pastry shell. Serve with a dry or flowery white Rioja.

Husarenfleisch [hoo-*zahr*-en-flysh]
This Austrian specialty is thin slices of veal, pork, and tenderloin sautéed with onions, first moistened with brown stock then sour cream, and served with boiled potatoes and beer.

Imbrogliata [eem-brohl-*yah*-tah]
Beaten eggs poured into a simmered-down sauce of tomatoes with garlic, peppercorns, and cloves, and served when the eggs are set. Artichokes or peppers are also used. Serve with a hearty red like Nebbiolo or a full, dry white like Soave.

Incasciata [een-kah-*shah*-tah]
A timbale of layers of *pasta*, beef or veal slices, and hard-boiled eggs. Serve with a white like Orvieto or a red like Bardolino.

Intingolo di lepre [een-*teen*-go-lo dee *leh*-preh]
Pieces of hare, sautéed in a casserole in butter and lard, then
stewed in red wine and stock, with a *bouquet garni,* onions,
mushrooms, artichoke hearts, and parsnips, with the mashed
liver of the hare. Serve with any full red wine, like Barolo.

Involtini [een-vohl-*tee*-nee]
Thin slices of veal rolled around a slice of ham and a leaf of
sage, stewed, or sautéed in butter; *alla maggiorana* (mahj-joh-
rah-nah) calls for a filling of salami and cheese seasoned with
marjoram. Serve with light red wine like Bardolino, or a dry
white like Soave or Orvieto.

Jambon à la crème [zhahm-bohn ah lah krem]
Slices of ham braised in dry white wine—Pouilly-Fumé or
Chablis, for instance—and served with the sauce blended with
veal stock and cream; *sous la cendre* (soo la sahn-druh) is a
small ham wrapped in puff paste, and baked; *en croûte* (on
kroot) employs bread dough for wrapping. Accompany with
dry white wines like the above.

Jungfernbraten [*yoonk*-fairn-brah-tn]
Pork tenderloin braised on browned onions and carrots, and
moistened with stock and sour cream, this sauce being strained
and finished with a little vinegar. Serve with Gumpoldskirchener or Rhine whites.

Kaiserfleisch [*ky*-zer-flysh]
Boiled rack of smoked and pickled pork, served with sauerkraut and bread dumplings or a pea purée. Serve with Austrian
whites or beer.

Kalbsbraten mit Bier [*kahlps*-brah-tn mit beer]
Roasted veal loin, cooked in an open pot with butter, onions,
and carrots, to which beer, bay, and cloves are added. Serve
with beer.

Kalbsgulyás [*kolps*-gool-yahs]
Veal goulash, the specialty of Vienna, varied in endless ways,
but often in white wine or stock, and with paprika, served with
dumplings or noodles and red or white wines.

Königsberger Klops [*keu*-neeks-bair-gur]
Meatballs of chopped beef and pork, anchovies and onions,
bound with bread and eggs, then simmered in stock, and served
in a sauce made of the stock and white wine, containing capers,
more chopped anchovies, mustard, and thinly sliced lemon,
thickened with eggs. Serve with beer or Steinwein.

Labskaus [*lahps*-kows]
Sailor's beef is pickled brisket boiled in seasoned stock, then
chopped and mixed with chopped fried onions, soaked salted
herring, and hot mashed potatoes, served with pickles, beets,
and beer.

Lämmernes Gebackenes [*lem*-er-nes guh-*bok*-nes]
Austrian specialty of squares of boned lamb shoulder, dipped
in egg and breaded, fried in lard, and served with lettuce
salad and beer or Austrian white wines.

Lamproie au vin [lahm-prwah oh van]
Lamprey browned in rye flour, then stewed in red wine with
mushrooms and green onions, laurel and thyme, is a Bordeaux
specialty, although *la lamproie aux poireaux* (pwah-roh) is
still more typical, leeks and parsley taking the place of the
mushrooms and onions, the pieces being served on fried toast.
Serve with Médoc or St. Émilion.

Langosta a la catalana [lon-*goh*-stah ah lah kah-tah-*lah*-nah]
Spiny lobster sautéed quickly in very hot oil, to which is added
tomatoes and peppers, then white wine, parsley, and saffron.
When this is reduced, cayenne pepper and brandy is added,
which is then set aflame and poured over the lobster chunks,
which are then decorated with croutons. Barcelona specialty,
along with *arroz parellada* (fried rice), *zarzuela de mariscos*
(thar-*thweh*-la deh mah-*rees*-kohs) (fried mollusks), and *tor-
tella de cabello de angel* (tor-*tehl*-ya deh ka-*behl*-yo deh *ahn*-
hel) (cakes of winter squash). Serve with dry or medium white
Rioja.

Langostinos a la vinagreta levantina [lon-go-*stee*-nohs ah lah vee-nah-*greh*-ta leh-vahn-*tee*-nah]
Cold boiled prawns, served with a vinaigrette to which has been added a mixture of diced eggs and onions, seasoned with cayenne and powdered saffron, then blended with brandy. Catalan specialty, along with fruits and cheeses. Serve with Fino or Manzanilla Sherries or white Rioja.

Langouste au naturel [lahn-goost oh nah-choor-el]
The spiny lobster, often called crawfish, is cooked in all the ways that lobster is, one Brittany fashion being to boil it in herbed water and serve it with coarse salt, buttered dark rye, and cider; the grilled lobster, first partially boiled in bouillon, then drenched with butter and grilled, is served with mayonnaise or vinaigrette. Accompany with Muscadet or other white wine.

Langue de bœuf [lahng duh buhf]
Ox tongue, simmered when smoked or pickled, boiled or braised after soaking in water, when fresh. Served with many garnishes, and frequently accompanied with light reds like Beaujolais, or white wines like Pouilly-Fuissé.

Langue de bœuf au gratin [lahng duh buhf oh grah-tan]
Tongue is usually boiled in seasoned water, but, additionally, cooked slices are served with various sauces. This version calls for laying slices on browned onions, adding white wine and bouillon, chopped mushrooms and crumbs, dotting with butter, then browning in the oven. Serve with flowery white wines of the Loire or Alsace.

Lapereau sauté au Champagne [lap-roh so-tay oh sham-pan-yuh]
Young rabbit is a French favorite, when sautéed and braised in Champagne with shallots, or when cooked in more complex fashion, like hare. Serve with red Burgundies or Rhônes.

Lapin à la bourbonnaise [la-pan ah lah boor-bon-nehz]
Wild rabbit sautéed with spring onions, then braised in Pouilly-Fumé with a *bouquet garni*, served on toast with the sauce

thickened with yolk and cream. Serve with red Chinon or Burgundies, particularly Pommard, or the Pouilly.

Lasagne [la-*zahn*-yeh]
Broad noodles served with sauce, as a luncheon dish or *pasta* course: *alla piemontese* is with a meat sauce and raw white truffles; *alla genovese* is classic, with *il pesto* sauce; *alla marchigiana* is baked in the oven with a meat stew and truffles; *alla napolitana* is with a meat sauce and layers of mozzarella cheese, hard-cooked eggs, and sausages; *alla bolognese* is green noodles served with meat sauce. Serve with red wines, light or full, like Chianti or Nebbiolo.

Lechoncito asado [leh-chon-*thee*-toh ah-*sah*-doh]
Roast suckling pig.

Lengua a la aragonesa [*lehn*-gwa ah lah ah-rah-go-*neh*-sah]
Aragon tongue is boiled, then simmered in an earthenware pot in olive oil and seasoned with chopped green peppers, onions, garlic, tomatoes, carrots, parsley, thyme, clove, and a little chocolate, finally garnished with sliced carrots. Serve with dry white Rioja.

Lenguado a la vasca [lehn-*gwah*-doh ah lah *vahs*-kah]
This sole or flounder dish is a Basque classic, the fish being set upon small potatoes in a pan, then baked lightly in olive oil, butter and lemon juice. The pan juices are blended with butter, chopped onions, mushrooms, and peppers, with some tomato, which is poured over the sole and finished in a very hot

oven. Navarra specialty, along with *chuletas de cordero* (choo-*leh*-tahs deh kor-*deh*-roh), lamb chops, *"cochifrito"* (koh-chee-*free*-toh) a lamb fricassee, and Roncal cheese. Serve with dry or flowery white Rioja.

Liebre estofada con judías [lee-*eh*-breh es-to-*fah*-da kon hoo-*dee*-ahs]
Hare stewed in an earthenware pot with wine, oil, and vinegar, and a *bouquet garni*, to which boiled string beans are added in the last few minutes, along with chopped red peppers sprinkled as a garnish over the whole just before serving. Cuenca specialty, along with *"morteruelo"* (mor-teh-*rweh*-lo), a pork liver fricasee; *guisado de cordero lechal* (ghee-*sah*-do deh kor-*deh*-ro leh-*chahl*), lamb ragout; and *morcillas* (mor-*theel*-yas), black pudding. Serve with red Rioja.

Lièvre à la bernardine [lee-ave-ruh ah lah bair-nahr-deen]
Hare braised on layers of bacon and herbs is drenched with *marc de Bourgogne* (mar), the sauce thickened with cream: *à la royale* is hare stuffed with the diced giblets, *foie gras,* chopped onions and garlic, truffles and parsley, bread crumbs and the blood, the whole stewed in white wine and served with a brandied game sauce. Serve with full Burgundies or Rhônes, particularly Pommard.

Lobster thermidor
Live lobster, split, then boiled or baked with olive oil, the meat removed then put back in the shells, covered with *sauce Bercy* to which mustard is added, sprinkled with cheese, and browned in the oven. Serve with full white wines like Meursault or Rhines.

Lomo de cerdo asado [*loh*-moh deh *thair*-doh ah-*sah*-doh]
Roast loin of pork.

Loncha de ternera [*lohn*-cha deh tare-*neh*-rah]
Veal steak breaded and sautéed in butter, then served with tomato sauce. Serve with red or white Rioja.

Loup grillé [loo gree-yay]
Loup is a rockfish, like a sea perch, and with *chapon* and *rouget* is considered among the finest of Mediterranean fish, generally grilled with olive oil then sprinkled with more oil and fennel, or sautéed in oil and covered with *sauce provençale*, crumbed and browned in the oven. Serve with Provence or Rhône whites and *rosés*.

Maccheroni [mok-keh-*roh*-nee]
The general name for a variety of tubular noodles made with egg, including *mezzani, rigatoni,* and *bucatini*. Macaroni is the Anglicized spelling that identifies the dry *pasta*, although the fresh is much better, particularly when cooked *al dente* (ahl *dehn*-teh), to the point where it is still bity. Dozens of sauces are used; *alla marinara* (mah-ree-*nah*-rah) of tomatoes, parsley, and garlic sautéed in oil; *alla pescatora* (pehs-kah-*toh*-rah) with anchovies, olives, and capers added to a *marinara; alla principe di Napoli* (*preen*-chee-peh dee *nah*-poh-lee) with chicken breasts, peas and mozzarella cheese in meat sauce; *alla carbonara* with ham, Parmesan cheese and beaten eggs sautéed in butter; *alla calbrese* (ka-lah-*breh*-zeh) with artichokes and cheese; *a tre dita* (ah treh *dee*-tah) with eggplant, chopped meat, cheese, cinnamon, and sugar; *alla siciliana* with sardines, pine kernels, and raisins, with fennel and saffron in oil. Serve with hearty red or white wines like Chianti or Orvieto.

Masthuhn nach Bauernart [*mahst*-hoon nok *bowrn*-art]
"Pullets peasant style" are made by dipping the parts in egg, then in grated cheese and bread crumbs, and sautéing them in butter. Button mushrooms are sautéed in the same butter with a squeeze of lemon, white wine is added; the sauce is thickened with yolks and poured over the chicken. Serve with a potato salad and beer or Rhine wine.

Médaillons de bœuf [meh-dy-yawn duh buhf]
Same as tournedos, steaks from the tenderloin, usually grilled and served with a variety of garnishes, accompanied with light reds like Médoc or Côte d'Or Burgundies.

Melanzone ripiene [meh-lahn-*tsah*-neh ree-*pyeh*-neh]
Eggplant stuffed with anchovies, olives, capers, and chopped onions and tomatoes, baked or stewed in a casserole is a particular favorite in southern Italy, but other ways include: *alla parmigiana* (par-mee-*jah*-nah), sautéing half-inch slices in oil, sprinkling a layer in a casserole with bread crumbs seasoned with chopped garlic and parsley and grated Parmesan, covering this with tomato sauce and mozzarella slices, then repeating the process and baking in a hot oven until the mozzarella is bubbling; *alla romana* (roh-*mah*-nah) calls for similar layering in a casserole, then baking, starting with meat sauce, then browned eggplant slices, then mozzarella, a sprinkling of grated Parmesan and chopped basil, more meat sauce, and repeat, using some tomato sauce with the last layer; *alla fiorentina* calls for thinner slices placed raw in a casserole with olive oil, alternating with layers of sliced tomatoes and mozzarella, and baked slowly. Serve with hearty reds or full whites like Nebbiolo or Soave.

Menestra de legumbres frescas [meh-*neh*-strah deh leh-*goom*-brehs *freh*-skas]
A variety of vegetables cooked in a broth, with ham, olive oil being added to smooth the dish, which is then topped with asparagus and poached eggs. Murcia specialty, along with *besugo a la murciana* (beh-*soo*-goh ah lah moor-thee-*ah*-nah), sea bream. Serve with white Rioja.

Messicani [mes-see-*kah*-nee]
Veal balls stuffed with chopped veal, pork, ham and cheese mixture that has been spiced with nutmeg and garlic, and sautéed in butter to which broth is added. Serve with any fruity or light wine, like red or white Valtellina.

Minestra maritata [mee-*neh*-strah mah-ree-*tah*-tah]
Generally, *minestre* are the hot first courses of a meal as opposed to *antipasto*; either soups, *pasta* in broth, or greens. The *maritata* (ma-ree-*ta*-tah) is a Campanian dish of pork chunks in a meat broth seasoned with ham bones, with chicory and

cabbage; *farricello* (far-ree-*chehl*-lo) is a Roman version in broth (*battuto*; baht-*too*-toh) with tomatoes and pork rind, thickened with flour. Serve with light wines like red Falerno or white Frascati.

Minestrone milanese [mee-neh-*stroh*-neh mee-lah-*neh*-zeh]
The most celebrated of the soups, served hot or cold, containing finely chopped vegetables and rice or *pasta*, differing from *zuppa* (*dzoop*-pah), which contains chunks of meat, fish, or vegetables. The Milan version is mostly green vegetables and rice, seasoned with tomatoes, bacon, parsley, and sage, with Parmesan in the dish and sprinkled over it when served; *genovese* has *il pesto* added, and often eggplant and mushrooms; *fiorentino* contains white beans and cabbage, red peppers, pork and tomatoes, poured over stale bread or toast. Serve with dry white wines like Soave or Orvieto.

Miroton de bœuf [mee-roh-tawn duh buhf]
Sliced boiled beef simmered in beef stock full of browned onions, then served with a lacing of vinegar or white wine. Accompany with a fruity red like Beaujolais.

Morue a la guingampaise [moh-rü ah lah gwan-gahm-payz]
Marinated filets of cod, dipped in batter, rolled in grated cheese, then fried: *à la morlaisienne* (mor-leh-zyen) calls for poached pieces of cod and lobster, covered with cream sauce and baked between two pancakes; elsewhere the fish is fried in oil, with onions, tomatoes, and so forth. Serve with dry whites like Muscadet.

Moules marinière [mool mah-reen-yair]
Mussels poached in cider with shallots and parsley, butter and cream: *à la crème* calls for mussels sautéed with onions and garlic, butter and cloves, in some white wine, with whipped cream mixed in, then browned in the oven; *farcie aux épinards* (farsee oh-zeh-pee-nar) is a Provence specialty, the mussels being stuffed with leeks, onions, and spinach, sprinkled with crumbs and olive oil, then browned. Serve with dry white wines like Muscadet or Hermitage.

Mozzarrella in carozza [mot-tsar-*reh*-lah een kah-*rot*-tsah]
Slices of this soft white cream cheese so basic a part of many Italian dishes are placed on slices of bread, then dipped in batter and fried. This Neapolitan favorite is served very hot, with white Capri or Ischia.

Navarin de mouton [nah-vah-ran duh moo-tawn]
A stew of breast of mutton, served with small onions and potatoes, or a variety of spring vegetables. Accompany with red wines like Médoc or light Burgundies.

Nierndl mit Hirn [neerndl mit heern]
Sliced and sautéed kidneys mixed with boiled brains that have been chopped and sautéed with onions, then sprinkled with parsley. Serve with Austrian whites or Rhines.

Noisette de porc aux pruneaux [nwah-zet duh porc oh prü-no]
The *noix* (nwah) or noisettes are generally small, round slices from the filet of lamb or veal, and are prepared like cuts from the filet of beef, but in the Touraine a specialty is this cut from pork, roasted with prunes. Serve with flowery white Vouvray or red Chinon.

Œufs Bercy [uhf bair-see]
Fried eggs with little sausages, often with parsley or a ring of tomato sauce: *à la dauphinoise* means eggs fried *en cocotte* (on ko-kot) with nutmeg and cream: *sur le plat à la Lorraine* (sür luh pla ah lah lor-rehn) means eggs broken over a bed of diced bacon and thin slices of Gruyère, with some fresh cream

in the whites, the whole baked in the oven: *au plat lyonnaise* means eggs on a bed of browned chopped onions with some cream. Fried eggs are prepared with all sorts of regional garnishes, but few such dishes go well with wines, except perhaps Champagne.

Œufs brouillés   [uhf brwee-yay]
Cream, chicken stock, gravies, sautéed mushrooms are often mixed with scrambled eggs, which are then served on slices of fried ham or toast, with various garnishes, but rarely with wines. *Œufs brouillés à l'antiboise* (ahn-tee-bwahz) are layers of scrambled eggs alternating with layers of sautéed summer squash in a casserole, covered with Parmesan and browned in the oven, then served with tomato sauce, but not with a wine, unless someone insists on Provence *rosé*.

Olivette de vitello   [oh-lee-*veht*-teh dee vee-*tehl*-lo]
Thin veal slices rolled around such fillings as anchovies and capers, or diced ham and truffles with Parmesan, then browned in butter and simmered in white wine. Serve with full whites like Soave or light reds like Bardolino.

Olla cordobesa   [*ohl*-yah kor-do-*beh*-sa]
"Cordovan stew" is chickpeas boiled with bacon, cabbage being added during the last minutes of cooking. Serve with dry white Rioja.

Olla podrida   [*ohl*-yah po-*dree*-dah]
The Spanish *pot-au-feu*, mostly chickpeas and hocks and feet from sheep, calves, and pigs, with hot sausages, the soup being served first, followed by the meat and any vegetables that have been added. Serve with any fresh young wine, preferably red Rioja.

Omble chevalier   [ohmbl sheh-val-yay]
The great lake fish of France, particularly from Lake Annecy, a sort of landlocked salmon, which is prepared like trout or salmon, often with *sauce Nantua*, which calls for crayfish. Serve with local whites of the Savoy, Chablis, or Meursault.

Omelette aux fines herbes [ohm-let oh feen zairb]

The classic French omelet, three or four eggs mixed with two or three tablespoonfuls of water, the mixture poured into a pan sizzling with butter, the eggs being pulled in from the sides of the pan until partly set, a quantity of chopped herbs—mostly parsley, but also chervil, tarragon, and chives—sprinkled over, the omelet then being rolled onto a plate. It should still be runny in the middle, and golden but not deeply browned on the outside. Omelets are filled with all sorts of mixtures, and served with a variety of garnishes, but most are made in the above fashion, although *de la Mère Poularde* (mehr poo-lard) is the Norman fashion of beating the yolks and eggs separately, with cream, so that the omelet is piled high. Few omelets taste good with wines, except perhaps a light flowery white from the Loire or Alsace.

Ortolans à la landaise [or-toh-lahnz ah lah lahn-dayz]

The most delicate of the small birds of France, the classic preparation is to roast them in tiny paper boxes near an open fire, nothing at all being added; they are salted and peppered when served, eaten in the fingers piping hot. *Ortolans rôtis* (roh-tee) calls for wrapping them in vine leaves and roasting them in a hot oven on a skillet wetted with salt water, then serving them on fried toast with lemon wedges. Serve with St. Émilion or other red wines of Bordeaux.

Ossobuco [oh-so-*boo*-ko]

Braised veal shank is a specialty of Milan, where it is often served with *gremolada* (greh-moh-*lah*-dah) sauce—white wine, lemon peel, garlic, rosemary and sage—and a risotto. It is one of the hearty glories of northern Italy, and the marrow is particularly good in this dish. Serve with full wines like Barolo or Nebbiolo.

Ouillade [wee-yahd]

An outstanding Catalan dish, pickled pork boiled with cabbage and various other herbs and vegetables, particularly garlic, served on slices of bread, with white beans cooked separately. Accompany with Bordeaux reds or white Roussillon.

Paella de campiña   [pah-*ehl*-yah deh kahm-*pee*-nya]
This country *paella* of Cordoba is rice with ham, sausage, bacon, and chicken, seasoned with black pepper, laurel, and roasted garlic. Cordoba specialty, along with various stews. Serve with dry red or white Rioja.

Paella valenciana   [pah-*ehl*-yah vah-lehn-thee-*ah*-nah]
The classic Valencia *paella*, which is cooked quickly in a special *paella* pan, wide and shallow, on the top of the stove over a brisk wood fire, traditionally contains eel, shellfish, and string beans, in rice. The name has been adopted for the saffron rice dish that contains chicken, mussels, shrimp, peas, pimiento, and the hot sausage called *chorizo* (choh-ree-thoh). All *paellas* should be prepared in the special pan on the top of the stove, the rice being cooked in the broth, and other ingredients being added in sequence, so that everything is done at once. *Chuletas a la parilla con ali-oli* (choo-*leh*-tahs ah la pa-*reel*-ya kon *ah*-li-*oh*-lee), grilled chops with mayonnaise and garlic sauce, are also a Valencia specialty. Serve with any Spanish wine, red or white, including the dry Fino or Manzanilla Sherries.

Palombacci   [pah-lohm-*boch*-chee]
Pigeons roasted on a spit are an Umbrian specialty in spring and fall during their migration. They are served with *la ghiotta* (*gyot*-tah), a pungent, ancient sauce that combines olives and anchovies with lemon peel and sage in oil and wine. Serve with reds like Chianti.

Panissa   [pah-*nees*-sa]
A risotto, moist rice cooked with salami, beans, and bacon. Serve with white Cortese, or a light red like Bardolino.

Pasta [*pah*-stah]

The Italian name for the noodle, which originally came from China, and which became so varied and excellent in Bologna that dishes made with it have become the second course in a traditional Italian meal. Made with flour and water or flour and eggs, and cut in various sizes and shapes from *foglie*, or sheets, the taste varies subtly with thickness and shape, which also govern the amount and heartiness of sauces with which the noodles are combined. Egg noodles like *fettuccine* or *tagliatelle*, a quarter-inch wide, are generally served with delicate sauces, but the thicker, wider *lasagne* call for heartier meat and tomato sauces. *Spaghetti, vermicelli,* and the other fine lengths of *pasta* are usually served with thin sauces, often containing pieces of meat, while the bigger tubes are stuffed, as are the squares of *ravioli*. They are served *asciutta* (ah-*shoot*-tah), or dry, when they are boiled and served with a sauce, or *in brodo*, when they are boiled and served in broth; they are also baked and used as layers in casseroles. When not a separate course, they accompany main dishes, as do *risotto, polenta,* or potatoes. They are generally served with white wines, like Orvieto or Soave, or light reds like Bardolino or Valpolicella.

Pasta e fasoi [*pah*-stah eh fah-*zoy*]

Pasta boiled in a soup of white beans and pork rind. Serve with a hearty white wine like Verdicchio or Frascati.

Pasta incasciata [*pah*-stah een-kah-*shah*-tah]

A Sicilian dish, *pasta* layers filled with stew, diced meat, slices of hard-boiled egg and grated cheese. Equally famous is *pasta alle sarde* (sar-deh), layers of long macaroni alternating with fennel and fresh sardines, cooked in oil, spiced with raisins, pine nuts, anchovies and saffron. Serve with dry white Zucco or red Etna or Faro.

Pasticciata [pah-*steech*-chah-tah]

A casserole consisting of layers of *lasagne*, each covered with a cream sauce to which some Bolognese meat sauce has been added, which is then sprinkled with diced ham and mozzarella and grated Parmesan, then baked in a hot oven until brown. Also the name for an Urbino beef stew with bacon and cloves, and for a simliar Milanese dish containing meat and ham, *polenta* and cheese. Serve with white Soave or Prosecco, or red Bardolino or Valpolicella.

Pâté de veau et jambon   [pah-tay duh voh ay zhahm-bohn]
Literally, *pâtés* are potted meats, fowl, or game, served hot or cold, perhaps something like our meat loaves, usually consisting of highly spiced layers of sliced, chunked, or minced meats in oblong pans lined with dough. A veal and ham pâté starts with a layer of finely diced bacon on the bottom of the crust, then a layer of ground stuffing meat bound with egg, then layers of ham, pork, and veal slices, and repeating, with occasional layers of truffle or mushrooms. The whole is baked in an oven, with or without a pastry topping. There are endless variations, depending on the fillings chosen, and they are invariably magnificent to serve with wine. Those made with fish and sea food call for white wines, but meat and game *pâtés* call for fine red Burgundies and Bordeaux, although many of the ham, chicken, and veal patties are delicious with Burgundy whites like Pouilly-Fuissé, Chablis, Meursault, or the Montrachets.

Pauchouse   [po-shooz]
The classic Burgundian stew of fresh-water fish, a *matelote* of pieces of carp and tench sautéed with garlic, onions, and bacon strips, then stewed in white wine, and served on toast. In Mâcon, the stock is thickened with yolks, cream, and butter. Serve with Pouilly-Fuissé or other white Burgundies.

Paupiettes de veau à l'alsacienne   [po-pyet duh voh ah lah al-zas-yen]
Thin slices of veal and ham spread with chopped mushrooms, then rolled, and braised in Sylvaner. These rolls are also made with other meats, and fish filets, and stuffed with various spicy fillings. Serve with Sylvaner or Traminer.

Pecho de ternera a la sevillana [peh-cho deh tair-*neh*-rah ah la seh-veel-*yah*-nah]
A stuffed breast of veal, served with a garnish of almonds and olives. Trimmings of the breast are sautéed, then sprinkled on an omelet, which is then topped with pickles, the whole being rolled in the breast, tied, then sautéed in oil. The meat roll is removed, a sauce is made by sautéing tomatoes, onions, and carrots in the oil left in the pan, with thyme, bay, and parsley. The meat and sauce are combined, covered with wine and some water in a casserole, and then finished in the oven. May be served cold, with red or white Rioja.

Perdices al modo de Alcántara [pair-*dee*-thehs al *moh*-do deh al-*kahn*-tah-rah]
Partridges stuffed with duck livers and truffles soaked in port, roasted and served with the reduced wine and more truffles. Caceres specialty, along with Montánchez ham. Serve with old red Rioja or Bordeaux.

Perdiz a la torero [pair-*deeth* ah la to-*reh*-ro]
"Bullfighter's partridge" is stuffed with the diced giblets, anchovies, and bacon, then braised with tomatoes and pimiento, seasoned with salt, black pepper, parsley, and white wine, then served with thin slices of sautéed ham. Cadiz specialty, along with sautéed fish, and local asparagus. Serve with dry Rioja, red or white.

Perdiz de capellán [pair-*deeth* deh kah-pehl-*yahn*]
"Chaplain's partridge" is pounded filet of veal on which slices of fresh ham and sausage are placed, which is rolled, tied, dredged with flour, sautéed in pork fat, then simmered in white wine. Baleares specialty, along with *tortilla de sardinas frescas* (*fres*-kahs) (fresh sardine omelet), and *fideos gordos con sobrasada* (fee-*deh*-ohs gor-dohs kon sob-rah-*sah*-dah) (macaroni and sausages). "Poor man's partridge" is magnificent with a dry Rioja, white or red.

Perdreau à la catalane [pair-dro ah lah kah-tah-lahn]
Young partridges—with giblet, ham, bread, and parsley stuffing

—browned in goose fat, then braised in white wine, with garlic and tomatoes, more ham and a *bouquet garni* added to make a sauce. Local bitter oranges are often braised with the partridge. Serve with Hermitage or Provence whites, or red Rhônes.

Perdrix à la bourguignonne [pair-dree ah lah boor-gheen-yawn]
Partridge roasted with mushrooms and onions, served with a sauce made with red Burgundy. Serve with full Burgundies like Nuits-St.-Georges or Chambertin.

Pernici allo zabaione [pair-*nee*-chee *ahl*-lo tsah-bah-*yo*-neh]
A Piedmont classic, roast partridge with a custardy sauce made of yolks, sugar, and Marsala; *stufato di pernici* (stoo-*fah*-toh) is stewed in a casserole with chopped carrots and onions, and a *bouquet garni*, in white wine; *marinata di pernici* (mah-ree-*nah*-tah) is slices of roast partridge marinated in stock, oil, and vinegar to which has been added chopped onions, herbs, and an egg yolk; *ai cavoli* (eye *ka*-voh-lee) is stewed in a casserole with cabbage, sausages, and cloves, often in white wine with herbs and carrots. Serve with any full white wine like Orvieto, or a red wine like Barolo.

Pescada blanca a la malagueña [pehs-*kah*-dah *blahn*-kah ah lah mah-lah-*gay*-nya]
Slices of poached hake served with a mayonnaise clarified with the water in which ˙the fish was cooked. Málaga specialty, along with *chanquetes fritos* (chahn-*keh*-tehs *free*-tohs) fried anchovies. Serve with dry or flowery white Rioja.

Pesce in zimino [*peh*-sheh een tsee-*mee*-noh]
Fish poached in a white wine sauce containing tomatoes, mushrooms, and rosemary, a specialty of Trieste; *al bianco*

(*byahn*-ko) is poached fish; *al cartoccio* (kar-*tawch*-choh) is fish baked in paper or foil. Serve with white wines like Soave or Orvieto.

Petti di pollo milanese [*pet*-tee dee *pohl*-lo]
Breasts of chicken, breaded then sautéed in oil and butter, the pan juice being poured over them, then sprinkled with parsley and served with lemon wedges. In Bologna, breasts browned in butter, then allowed to simmer in white wine and stock, are finished by topping them with slices of ham and mozzarella and slipping them under the broiler. Truffles are usually added in the north. Serve with light reds like Bardolino or a white like Soave.

Pfeffer Potthast [*fef*-fer *pot*-hahst]
The "pepper pot" is generally chunks of chuck, sliced onions, bay, and herbs simmered in water, the stock thickened with bread crumbs and heavily peppered. Serve with beer.

Picadillo de lujo [pee-kah-*deel*-yo deh *loo*-ho]
Corned-beef hash.

Piccioni selvaticci [peech-*choh*-nee sel-*vah*-tee-chee]
Wild pigeons stewed in an earthenware pot, with oil and vinegar, olives, chopped onions and ham, cloves and sage, served with a sauce made from the pot liquor to which the mashed giblets, capers, and parsley have been added. Serve with full red wines like Barolo or Valtellina.

Piche-pache [peesh-pash]
Spanish turkey stew, chopped giblets being browned with onion and garlic, then boiled with cabbage, turnips, carrots, potatoes, and marrow, and served with tomato sauce. Serve with red or white Rioja.

Piemontese [pyeh-mawn-*teh*-zeh]
The northern Italian province—home of most of the best red wines—whose name on a dish generally indicates that it contains white truffles, the other specialty of the country.

Pipérade [pee-pair-odd]
A Basque specialty, pimiento or peppers, and tomatoes, onions, and garlic, added to lightly scrambled eggs, served with the entrée.

Pistache [pee-stash]
Denotes dishes cooked with garlic cloves when called *en pistache*, or with pistachio nuts when listed *aux pistache*.

Pizza [*peet*-tsah]
This Neapolitan specialty—which is basically a large round of bread dough covered with anchovies, cubes of mozzarella, tomatoes seasoned with oregano and a few drops of oil, which is baked to bubbling in a hot oven—has hundreds of variations. Serve with beer or a dry white wine like Capri or Vernaccia.

Poitrine de mouton farcie [pwah-treen duh moo-tawn far-see]
Rolled breast of mutton, usually stuffed with bacon or ham, herbs, bread soaked in milk or bouillon, then braised with carrots and onions, and stewed in stock or white wine and finished in the oven. Serve with light reds like Bordeaux.

Polenta [po-*lehn*-tah]
Corn-meal mush—yellow or white—often served hot and thin, with a sauce, or cooled and in squares, in place of rice or *pasta*. In Lombardy and the north it is the classic accompaniment for small game birds and salty meats. Serve with dry white wines like Soave, or light red wines like Valtellina.

Polenta i ösei [po-*lehn*-tah ee uh-zay]
"Mush and thrush" is one of the autumn excitements in Lombardy, particularly Bergamo, and while the name loses redolence in translation, the steamy mound of corn meal crowned with skewers of tiny birds scented with sage is a glory of Italian cuisine, so memorable that it is copied in pastry all year to remind everyone of the harvest splendor. Serve with red wines like Valtellina or Valpolicella, or with whites like Soave or Orvieto.

Polenta pasticciatta [po-*lehn*-tah pahs-tee-*chaht*-tah]
Corn-meal mush baked in a casserole, containing chopped meats and sausages, cheese and mushrooms, with white truffles. A luncheon dish, or accompaniment to a main course. Serve with any fruity light wine, red or white, like Valtellina.

Pollo al chilindrón [*pol*-yo al chee-leen-*drohn*]
Pieces of chicken sautéed in hot oil, with garlic cloves, with some chopped ham and onions added, then red pepper strips and tomatoes. Zaragosa specialty along with various cod dishes. Serve with the local Cariñena, or red Rioja.

Pollo alla diavola [*pohl*-lo *ahl*-la *dyah*-vo-lah]
Deviled chicken is a specialty in Tuscany, where the chicken is split and grilled, with oil and butter seasoned with ginger, onions, and parsley; *alla padovana* (pah-doh-*vah*-nah) is stewed in giblet gravy, diced onions, yolks, and lemon juice; *alla romana* is pieces stewed in dry white wine with ham, garlic, tomatoes, and tomato sauce; *alla cacciatore* (kah-chah-*tor*-eh) is hunter style, pieces sautéed in olive oil, with green peppers, tomatoes, onions, and mushrooms; *alla contadina* (kon-tah-*dee*-nah) is country style, sautéed in butter with rosemary, to-matoes, and garlic; *in padella* (pah-*dehl*-lah) is pan-fried pieces of ham and chicken, with tomatoes and peppers, marjoram, garlic, moistened with wine; *ripieno arrosto* (ree-*pyeh*-no ar-*rost*-oh) is roast chicken stuffed with veal, ham, tongue, Parme-san cheese, and bread crumbs moistened with Marsala; *imbot-tito* (im-boht-*tee*-to) is stuffed with ham, Romano cheese, and bread crumbs seasoned with marjoram and parsley. Serve with dry white wines like Soave, or light or fruity red wines like Nebbiolo or Bardolino.

Polpettine [pohl-peh-*tee*-neh]
Meat balls, a Milanese specialty, seasoned with nutmeg and *gremolada*—which is a mixture of chopped parsley, garlic, and lemon peel—sautéed in oil; *alla neapolitana* calls for ground pork and veal, as well as beef, and chopped raisins as well as parsley, the small cakes being often coated with bread crumbs

before being browned in butter. Serve with a red wine like Inferno or Vesuvio.

Porchetta [por-*keht*-tah]
Suckling pig, stuffed with garlic and rosemary, then roasted whole on a spit, is a favorite in the Umbrian hill towns. Serve with a light red wine like Chianti, or a dry white Orvieto.

Pot-au-feu [pawt-oh-fuh]
The classic dish of French country cookery, a pot kept a-simmer on the back of the stove, constantly replenished, now generally made by boiling rump beef and marrow bones with root vegetables and herbs, with onions and leeks, although anything may be added. Should be devoured wherever available and drunk with whatever is offered.

Pote gallego [*po*-teh gahl-*yeh*-go]
The Galician pot is made by boiling beef, ham and bacon, sausage and black pudding in salted water, then adding to this boiled cabbages and string beans, finally boiling potatoes in the mixture, then serving separately the broth, the cabbages and what's left. An Orense specialty. Serve with red Rioja, or the local Ribero.

Potée auvergnate [paw-tay oh-vairn-yat]
The *potée* is like a *pot-au-feu*, but can mean anything cooked in a pot, basically pork and cabbage, and frequently containing forcemeat seasoned with garlic and clove, bound with egg and wrapped in cabbage leaves, first poached in the stock, then baked. Serve on toast, with beer or local wines.

Poularde truffée à la périgourdine [poo-lard troof-fay ah lah pay-ree-goor-deen]
Although the best French pullets come from Bresse, local birds are used in Périgord, where they are stuffed with truffles and *foie gras* doused with Cognac, left in a covered pot with sautéed truffle peelings for a couple of days, then roasted, the sauce made from the pan gravy laced with Madeira; *à la toulousaine* (too-loo-zehn) is pullet stuffed with browned sausage, chopped liver and olives, onions, tomatoes, and garlic, braised in white wine, served with mushroom-stuffed tomatoes and eggplant: *demi-deuil* (duh-mee-deu-yuh), or half-mourning, is truffled pullet poached with leeks and carrot, served with the cleared, reduced stock or *sauce suprême*, truffles cooked in Madeira, and sweetbreads. (It is also called *poularde à la lyonnaise* or *poularde de Madame Filloux*.) Serve with fine red Burgundy or Bordeaux.

Poule au pot [pool oh po]
Chicken in the pot is a Gascon dish, the fowl stuffed with its chopped liver and ham, with beaten eggs, bread, and some garlic, herbs, and nutmeg, moistened with Armagnac and bouillon, then dangled on the end of a cord *à la ficelle* (fee-sel) in bouillon, or cooked in the bouillon with cabbage leaves filled with the stuffing. Serve with red Bordeaux or local wines.

Poulet de Bresse à la crème [poo-lay de bres ah la krem]
Young Bresse chickens slowly sautéed, then poached lightly in heavy cream, the sauce thickened with yolk and lemon juice; *à la champenoise* (shahmp-nwahz) is stuffed chicken lightly stewed in Champagne and garlic, then breaded and grilled; *en meurette* (on meu-ret) is a Burgundy specialty, the chicken poached in red wine with garlic and bacon, onions and mushrooms, parsley and thyme, then served on garlic toast; *à la niçoise* (nee-swahz) is chicken braised in olive oil and saffron, then poached in white wine and bouillon with a *bouquet garni*, olives, tomatoes, and garlic; *à la savoyarde* (sa-vwah-yard) is braised chicken doused with brandy then poached with mushrooms and served with the thickened sauce. Ordinary chickens

are often sautéed *basquaise* (bas-kehz), with peppers, tomatoes, and garlic, or hunter style, *chasseur* (sha-suhr) with mushrooms and bacon. Serve with whites like Pouilly-Fuissé or reds like Beaujolais.

Pré-sâlé [pray-sah-lay]
Lamb raised on the salt marshes of Brittany and Normandy, with an inimitable and delicate savor, the name appearing alone generally signifying a simply roasted leg of lamb, usually served with the white beans of Brittany. Accompany with a fine red Bordeaux of the Médoc or Graves.

Puchero madrileña [poo-*cheh*-ro mah-dree-*leh*-nya]
The national soup of Spain, a refined Madrid version includes chicken as well as the usual beef brisket, ham or bacon, and *chorizos*—along with chickpeas, tomatoes, and green peppers—dumplings of potato or ground ham or bacon being added just before serving. Serve with a light red or white Rioja.

Quenelles de brochet [kuh-nell duh broh-sheh]
Dumplings are made of any mashed and bound fish, fowl, or meat, and are poached in various stocks, but the most famous is mashed creamed pike from Nantua, fish puffs so delicate and light that they have become one of the outstanding creations of modern French cuisine, to be served with fine dry whites like Corton or Montrachet.

Queue de bœuf [keu duh buhf]
Oxtail, generally stewed in white wine or stock, and served with a variety of garnishes. Generally accompanied with hearty red wines like Rhônes, or Beaujolais.

Ragout de mouton [rah-goo de moo-tawn]
Although stews are made out of almost anything, mutton with onions and potatoes and herbs is the most common, and something of a specialty in northern France, where it is accompanied with red wines like Beaujolais. Fish stews call for white wines.

Ragù bolognese [rah-*goo* bo-lo-*nyeh*-zeh]
This rich and hearty stewlike sauce is used with all varieties of

pasta, and is basically chopped beef and lean pork—and sometimes veal, ham, and bacon—added to sautéed and chopped onion, celery, and carrots, simmered in stock, white wine, and tomato paste. Mushrooms, chicken livers, and cream are often added to make the sauce still richer. It is one of the great, classic sauces of Italy. The Neapolitan version calls for a pot roast instead of stew meat. Serve with fruity reds like Barolo.

Ratatouille   [rah-tah-tooy]
A familiar Provence dish of tomatoes, eggplant, and summer squash stewed together with olive oil and garlic, and served with all manner of Provence dishes, particularly roasts and grillades. It is especially appetizing with lamb and fish.

Ravioli alla genovese   [rah-*vyoh*-lee *ahl*-lah jeh-no-*veh*-zeh]
One of the most famous Italian dishes, *pasta* squares filled with mashed chicken, veal, and other delicacies, with beets and both ricotta and Parmesan cheese, well-seasoned with borage. There are many other raviolis, generally best with red wines like Chianti.

Reindibiftek   [*ryn*-dee-beef-tek]
Austrian potted tenderloin steak, browned, then braised in *demi-glace,* served with a fried egg on top, sliced gherkins, and slices of boiled potato lightly browned in butter. Serve with fruity reds like Beaujolais.

Rillettes de Tours   [ree-yet duh toor]
Shredded pork cooked in little pots, in lard, to be spread on bread, the perfect accompaniment to Vouvray.

Rindfleisch gedämpft in Bier   [*rint*-flysh guh-*demft* in beer]
Beef with vegetables stewed in a Dutch oven in beer, and usually served with beer.

Riñones al Jerez   [ree-*nyo*-nehs al hare-*eth*]
One of the simplest glories of Spanish cuisine, thin slices of lamb kidney are sautéed in olive oil over a hot fire, Fino or Amontillado Sherry is added, the kidneys are stirred quickly then served piping hot, by themselves, with toast or scrambled

eggs, or whatever. The traditional recipe calls for a brown gravy, preferably veal, to be added with the Sherry. Chicken livers can also be cooked this way, being generously sprinkled with parsley when served. Accompany with a red or white Rioja, a good Burgundy or Bordeaux.

Ris de veau dauphinoise [ree dvoh do-feen-wahz]
Calf's sweetbread sautéed, served with a sauce of gravy, lemon juice, and butter containing chopped shallots, tomatoes, and parsley. Serve with Beaujolais.

Risi e bisi [*ree*-see eh *bee*-see]
A Venetian luncheon dish, thick soup of rice and peas, seasoned with onions and celery, bacon and ham. Serve with a light white wine like Soave.

Risi e peoci [*ree*-zee eh peh-o-chee]
A Venetian *risotto*, with mussels or clams. Serve with a dry white like Orvieto.

Riso [*ree*-zo]
Like a *risotto*, boiled rice with which various chopped meats and vegetables are cooked. Accompanies a main dish, usually.

Risotto alla milanese [ree-*zoht*-toh *ahl*-lah mee-lah-*neh*-zeh]
Saffron rice cooked in white wine and chicken stock with marrow and chopped onions, generally served with meat or fowl. When substantial amounts of meat or fish are added to the risotto, it can be a hearty main course; *alla piemontese* (pih-eh-mon-*teh*-zeh) is rice boiled in butter—with that mark of

Piedmont cuisine, the white truffle—and served with a meat sauce; *alla certosina* (chair-toh-*see*-nah) contains shrimp, and sometimes crayfish or mussels or fish, and mushrooms and peas; *alla toscana* (tos-*kah*-nah) contains chicken livers and is cooked in meat stock; *alla padovana* (pah-do-*vah*-nah) contains chopped veal, chicken giblets, mushrooms and marrow, with a tomato sauce, while *alla bechera* and *alla sbirraglia* (zbeer-*ahl*-ya) contain much the same ingredients as the Paduan version. All of them are served with grated Parmesan cheese, and taste best with the local Italian red wines.

Rissoles [rees-sohl]
These are small fried pastries filled with spicy meats, usually chicken or turkey combined with ham and mushroom, with seasonings, and bound with yolk, milk-soaked bread, or gravy. *Rissoles de St. Flour* (san fluhr) are filled with cheeses, eggs, chopped chervil, and chives. Serve with Beaujolais or light reds from Burgundy's Côte de Beaune, or Bordeaux.

Rognons de veau sautés [roh-nyon duh voh soh-tay]
Calf's kidneys are the most popular, although lamb, mutton, and beef kidneys are also used, usually sautéed with shallots, mushrooms, ham, tomatoes, or other flavoring ingredients. They are occasionally grilled, to be served with chops or steaks. Serve with full red wines like Beaujolais.

Rostbraten [*rohst*-brah-tn]
Austrian sirloin steak—less than an inch thick and pounded— usually pan-fried or stewed. *Dämpfrostbraten* (dempf-) is steak placed on a bed of lightly sautéed chopped onions in a Dutch oven, covered with raw peas, asparagus tips, mushrooms, and other spring vegetables, with some stock and butter, and stewed in a covered pan in the oven; *Pressburger Rostbraten* (*pres*-boorg-er) is stewed in cream sauce and covered with peas and egg slices; *Maschinrostbraten* (mah-*sheen*-) is sautéed in butter, then stewed with onions, potatoes, and paprika; *Zigeuner* (tsih-*gheu*-ner) is browned with bacon and onions, then stewed in brown gravy with marjoram, cabbage, and potatoes. There

are many other ways of preparation; generally served with fruity reds like Beaujolais or beer.

Rouget à la nicoise   [roo-zhay ah lah nee-swahz]
Red gurnet is generally sautéed, but this version calls for grilling it after sprinkling it with olive oil, then covering it with chopped mushrooms and truffles, onions and shallots, bread crumbs and a sprinkle of white wine, then baking it, or sautéing it in oil on dice of tomatoes. Serve with local Provence whites or *rosés*.

Rouladen   [roo-*lah*-den]
Beef rolls braised in bouillon, sometimes first stuffed with a little chopped onion, gherkins, and raw bacon, served in the pan gravy seasoned with a *bouquet garni*. Serve with beer.

Rusticiana   [roo-stee-*chah*-nah]
This far from "country" dish is a loin of veal or pork, with sausages, braised in a casserole with tomato and onions, seasoned with a little white wine, sage, and rosemary. Serve with a fruity red wine like Valgella or Inferno.

Salmis de palombe   [sahl-mee duh pah-lohm]
Salmis are dishes usually of wildfowl or small game, that are partially finished at the table; in this case, roasted or baked slices of wild dove, mixed with onions and shallots that have been chopped and browned, or with mushrooms and truffles, are served on fried toast with a sauce of the juices, cream, and the pounded innards. The slices are often flamed, wines and spices are generally added to the sauce. Very rich, these dishes call for full wines like St. Émilions or Côte d'Or Burgundies.

Salmorejo de perdiz a la toledana   [sahl-mo-*reh*-ho deh pair-*deeth* ah lah toh-leh-*dah*-nah]
A partridge custard, surrounded with the breasts, then bathed in salmi sauce. Toledo specialty, along with sautéed rabbit. Serve with red Rioja.

Saltimbocca alla romana   [sahl-teem-*bok*-kah]
A Roman classic, thin slices of veal sautéed in butter with ham

and sage. Serve with light white wines like Frascati, or light reds like Bardolino.

Sancocho canario [san-*cho*-cho kah-*na*-ree-oh]
Salted fish, boiled with tomatoes, served with *mojo* (*moh*-ho) a red sauce made with peppers, garlic, cumin, oil, and vinegar. Las Palmas specialty, along with *puchero de siete carnes* (poo-*cheh*-ro deh see-*eh*-teh *kar*-nehs), a meat stew, and *gofio canario* (*goh*-fyo), baked corn meal. Serve with young red or white Rioja.

Sardines grillées [sar-deen gree-yay]
Fresh sardines in Brittany are grilled, buttered, and served with boiled potatoes; in Nice they are dipped in beaten eggs, crumbed, then grilled and served with black olives. In both places they are accompanied with dry white wines like Muscadet or Bellet.

Sartù di riso [sar-*too* dee *ree*-zo]
A Neapolitan timbale filled with meat balls and sausages, tomatoes and mushrooms and mozzarella, covered with tomato sauce and bread crumbs, then oven-browned. Serve with red Gragnano or Ravello.

Sauces
Sauces distinguish, and lend their names to, many dishes of French and other cuisines. Basic sauces are made by adding to stock or gravy—*fond* (fohn) or *jus de viande* (zhü duh vyahnd)—or to the boiled-down essence or glaze of these rich liquids—*fumet* (fü-meh) or *glace de viande* (glas). Often added for richness are: a *roux* (roo)—paste of flour and butter; a *mirepoix* (meer-pwah)—dice of carrot, onion, bacon, celery, bay, and thyme; a *bouquet garni* (boo-keh gar-nee)— basically, a bundle of celery, parsley, thyme, and bay; and various butters that have been blended with mashed herbs, anchovy, lobster coral, crayfish, or other flavorsome ingredients. Sauces are usually bound—*lié* (lee-ay)—with butter, cream, or yolks. The basic sauces, called "mother sauces," are:

Allemande [al-mahnd] is a thickened veal stock enriched with white stock and mushroom stock, seasoned with white pepper and lemon juice, thickened more with beaten egg yolks.

Béchamel [beh-shah-mel] is a white sauce, made by simmering white *roux* in milk with onions, seasoning with nutmeg, salt, and white pepper, enriching with cream.

Demi-glace [duh-mee-glas] is a brown sauce made by adding veal gravy to *sauce espagnole*, along with tomato paste, ham parings, and mushroom peelings, then boiling down to desired thickness.

Espagnole [es-pah-nyohl] is beef stock, brown *roux* and brown *mirepoix*, to which is added a *bouquet garni* and peppercorns, slowly boiled down to desired thickness.

Hollandaise [ol-ahn-dayz] or Dutch sauce is egg yolk beaten with watered vinegar in a double boiler until slightly thick, to which is added white pepper, then butter, salt, cayenne, and lemon juice.

Suprême [sü-prem] is poultry stock and mushroom stock reduced, to which thickened chicken stock and fresh cream is added, it then being reduced again.

Tomate [toh-mat] is tomato paste to which is added *mirepoix* and bacon browned in butter; this is reduced in the oven, where it is sprinkled with flour, then are added stock, garlic, a *bouquet garni*, salt, sugar, and peppercorns, with some butter at the end.

Velouté [vuh-loo-tay] or velvet sauce is made by adding *roux* to various stocks simply to thicken them: *velouté de veau* is based on white stock; *velouté de volaille* (voh-ly-uh) is based on chicken stock; *velouté de poisson* (pwah-sohn) is based on fish stock; *velouté de légumes* (leh-güm) is based on vegetable stock.

Africaine [af-ree-kehn]
Spicy brown sauce with cayenne and diced truffles, laced with Madeira.

Aioli [eye-oh-lee]
Provençal mayonnaise with crushed garlic, lovingly used on vegetables, eggs, fish, and lobster.

Albert [al-bair]
Horseradish and English mustard in German or butter sauce.

Albuféra [al-bü-fair-ah]
Sauce suprême spiced with meat glaze and pimiento butter.

Alexandra
Hot *sauce suprême* with truffles, or cold mayonnaise with English mustard, chopped chervil, egg yolks.

Allemande [al-mahnd]
A basic sauce, a thickened white sauce, further enriched with veal stock, laced with lemon juice, and finally thickened with egg yolks.

Américaine [a-mehr-ee-kehn]
Hot thickened fish stock with pounded lobster coral, butter and tomato sauce, or cold mayonnaise with lobster purée and mustard.

Amiral [a-mee-ral]
White fish sauce with anchovy butter, grated lemon rind, and capers.

Ancienne [ahn-syen]
Hollandaise with chopped gherkins, truffles, mushrooms.

Andalouse [ahn-dah-looz]
Mayonnaise blended with tomato purée, red peppers.

Apfelkren [*ahp*-fuhl-krehn]
Grated apple and horseradish with Austrian white wine, paprika, sugar and vinegar.

Arlésienne [ahr-leh-zyen]
Sauce béarnaise with tomato purée, anchovy paste, and chopped tomatoes.

List of sauces (continued)

Aromates [ah-ro-mat]

A *bouquet garni* reduced in white wine, strained and enriched with *demi-glace* or fish *velouté*, and chopped chervil.

Aurore [oh-roar]

A thickened fish or veal stock colored with tomato purée, and laced with butter.

Avignonnaise [ah-vee-nyawn-ehz]

Cream sauce with Parmesan cheese, garlic, and chopped parsley.

Bagna cauda [*bahn*-yah *kow*-dah]

One of Italy's greatest sauces, a hot bath into which raw vegetables and other bits of food are dipped, it is a blend of oil, butter, and garlic, with truffles and minced anchovies. Magnificent with all sorts of drinks.

Bâtarde [ba-tard]

Creamy butter sauce with fish stock.

Bavaroise [ba-var-wahz]

Hollandaise with crayfish butter.

Béarnaise [beh-ar-nehz]

Egg yolks and butter, with shallots and tarragon, beaten in a double boiler until thick, cayenne and lemon juice, chopped tarragon and chervil, being added. A classic sauce for steaks and grillades.

Béchamel [beh-shah-mel]

Cream sauce.

Bercy [bair-see]

Chopped shallots in butter with white wine—reduced with fish stock for a fish sauce, meat glaze for meats—and chopped parsley added at the last.

Beurre noir [buhr nwahr]

Butter darkly browned, with a little vinegar.

Bigarrade [bee-gar-rahd]

Stock from a duck, flavored with orange juice and julienne of orange rind and lemon.

Bonne femme [bun fam]

White cream sauce with white wine, chopped mushrooms and shallots.

List of sauces (continued)

Bonnefoy [bun-fwah]
Like a *sauce bordelaise* but with white wine and *velouté*, and with chopped beef marrow and tarragon.

Bordelaise [bord-lehz]
Chopped shallots, thyme, nutmeg, and pepper, reduced in red Bordeaux, with *demi-glace* and whipped butter added, or a moistened *mirepoix*.

Bourgeoise [boor-zhwahz]
Brown sauce reduced with red wine, chopped mushroom and onion.

Bourguignonne [boor-gheen-yon]
Chopped shallots, thyme, laurel, parsley, and mushroom peelings, reduced in red Burgundy, with whipped butter and cayenne added. *Demi-glace* is often added.

Bressane [bres-san]
Spanish-style sauce flavored with orange juice and chopped chicken livers.

Bretonne [bruh-ton]
White wine or cream sauce made with onions, butter, and a julienne of leeks, carrots, and celery or tomato and parsley.

Broglie [brohl-yeh]
Demi-glace reduced with mushroom stock, with Oloroso Sherry or Madeira, and diced ham.

Bulgare [bül-gar]
Cold tomato sauce, often thickened with mayonnaise, with finely cut cooked celery.

Byron
Red wine sauce with julienne of truffles.

Cambridge
A sort of mayonnaise made by rubbing through a sieve hard-boiled yolks, capers, and anchovies, dill and tarragon, then beating in olive oil, adding mustard, cayenne, vinegar, and chopped parsley.

Cardinal
Cream sauce with fish essence and crushed lobster coral, cayenne and truffles.

Casanova

Mayonnaise with truffles and hard-boiled eggs.

Castellane

Demi-glace with finely chopped pimiento and ham, flavored with Oloroso Sherry, Madeira or lemon juice.

Chantilly [shahn-tee-yee]

Hot mayonnaise or cream sauce enriched with whipped cream; or cold hollandaise with whipped cream.

Charcutière [shar-kü-tyair]

Finely sliced gherkins added to *sauce Robert*.

Chasseur [sha-suhr]

Sauté of shallots and mushrooms, reduced with white wine then *demi-glace*, with chopped parsley to finish.

Châteaubriand [sha-toh-bree-ahn]

Shallots and mushrooms reduced in white wine, thyme, and bay, strained and blended with *demi-glace* and butter, finished with chopped parsley.

Chaud-froid [shoh-frwah]

Thick reduced stock with aspic and cream, that can be made green with spinach, pink with tomato purée or crayfish or lobster butter, blond with meat glaze. For *chaud-froid brune* (brün), *demi-glace* is used.

Cherbourg [shair-boor]

Cream sauce with crayfish butter and crayfish tails.

Chevreuil [sheh-vreu]

Poivrade sauce reduced with red wine, spiced with cayenne.

Choron [sho-rawn]

Sauce béarnaise with tomatoes.

Colbert [kohl-bair]

Meat or fowl essence whipped with butter and lemon juice, nutmeg and cayenne, with chopped parsley and Madeira added, or chopped tarragon.

Créole
Light sauté of shallots or onions, reduced with white wine, then blended with tomato sauce.

Cumberland
Currant jelly, Port, and orange juice, with mustard, cayenne, and ginger, reduced, then blended with brown sauce, with a julienne of orange and lemon peel, blanched shallots.

Demi-deuil [duh-mee-deuy]
Half-mourning sauce is thickened chicken or veal stock, with truffles.

Demi-glace [duh-mee-glas]
A brown sauce made by adding veal gravy to *sauce espagnole*, along with tomato paste, ham parings, and mushroom peelings, then boiling down to desired thickness.

Diable [dyahbl]
Shallot sauté reduced with white wine and vinegar, then reduced further after adding *demi-glace* and a *bouquet garni*. A second version is made by then adding Worcestershire and Harvey sauces, with some cayenne.

Diane [dee-an]
Sauce poivrade enriched with cream, with diced truffle.

Diplomate [dee-plo-mat]
Cream sauce with lobster butter, diced truffle, and lobster.

Duchesse [dü-shes]
Cream sauce with a dice of tongue and mushroom.

Duxelles [du-sel]
A sauté of diced mushroom, shallot, and onion, reduced with white wine, then blended with brown sauce and tomato purée, and simmered with chopped parsley for a few minutes.

Écossaise [eh-ko-sehz]
Scotch sauce is a cream sauce with chopped hard-boiled egg whites and sieved yolks.

Épicurienne [eh-pee-kür-yen]
Hot white sauce with vinegar, cayenne, and ketchup, or mayonnaise blended with cucumber purée and chutney.

Espagnole [es-pa-nyol]
A basic sauce of brown stock, *roux*, and *mirepoix*, reduced with a *bouquet garni* and peppercorns.

Fermière [fair-myair]
A fondue of slivers of carrot, turnip, celery knob, and onions or leeks, lightly sautéed, then blended with a cream sauce. More an accompaniment for grillades and so forth, than an actual sauce.

Financière [fee-nahn-syair]
Demi-glace flavored with Madeira and truffle essence.

Flamande [fla-mahnd]
A buttery cream sauce, or melted butter, with mustard, lemon juice, and chopped parsley.

Foyot [foy-oh]
Sauce béarnaise with meat glaze.

Française [frahn-sehs]
Sauce béarnaise with tomato purée and fish essence.

Garibaldi [gar-ee-*bahl*-dee]
Rich brown sauce flavored with mustard, cayenne, and garlic, beaten with anchovy butter.

Gastronome
Demi-glace reduced with Champagne, with cayenne.

Genevoise [zhuh-nuh-vwahz]
A sautée of salmon parts and *mirepoix*, reduced in red wine, with *demi-glace* added, then beaten with anchovy butter.

Gloucester
Mayonnaise with sour cream, mustard, Worcestershire sauce, and chopped fennel or tarragon.

Godard [go-dar]
A *mirepoix* and diced ham reduced in white wine, then reduced further with *demi-glace* and mushroom essence.

Gourmandise [goor-mahn-deez]
Brown sauce boiled with fish essence, then mixed with lobster butter and a dice of lobster and truffles.

Grand Veneur [grahn ven-uhr]
Sauce poivrade with venison glaze, currant jelly and cream.

Gribiche [grih-beesh]
Hard-boiled egg yolks beaten with mayonnaise, with the sliced whites, chopped gherkins, parsley, tarragon, chervil and capers being added. For cold fish.

Hollandaise
A basic sauce, egg yolks whisked with vinegar over a water bath, butter, cayenne and lemon being added.

Holstein
Cream sauce reduced with fish stock and white wine, seasoned with nutmeg and thickened with yolks.

Hongroise [ohn-grwahz]
White wine sauce blended with veal glaze, sour cream, and paprika; or chopped onions browned in paprika butter, reduced with a *bouquet garni* and white wine, then blended with *sauce suprême*.

Hussarde [üs-sard]
Chopped onions and shallots reduced in butter and white wine, to which is added white stock, tomatoed *demi-glace*, a bouquet and browned ham, strained, then sprinkled with horseradish, parsley and the ham.

Il Pesto [eel *peh*-sto]
The classic sauce of Genoese cooking, used to flavor all sorts of *pasta* and soups, is a pungent green sauce of basil and oil, with diced garlic, pine nuts, and cheese. Accompany with whites like Orvieto.

Indienne [an-dyen]
Sauce allemande or mayonnaise, with curry; or a sauté of onion and apple reduced with a curried *velouté*.

Ivoire [ee-vwhar]
Sauce suprême and veal *velouté* blended with meat glaze.

Joinville [zhwan-veel]
A fish sauce made with shrimp and crayfish stock and a julienne of truffles, added to *sauce normande*.

Lagupière [lah-gü-pyair]
Butter sauce with fish glaze and lemon juice, or *sauce normande* with chopped truffles and Madeira.

List of sauces (continued)

Livournaise [lee-voor-nehz]
Anchovy paste with chopped parsley and hard-boiled yolk, nutmeg and pepper, oil and vinegar.

Lyonnaise [lee-awn-ehz]
Sauté of onions reduced with game stock or meat glaze and veal stock, with chopped tarragon, nutmeg, lemon juice, butter, and more glaze.

Madère [mah-dair]
Demi-glace with Madeira, and, sometimes, tomato purée.

Maintenon [mant-nawn]
Sauce soubise with egg yolks.

Maître d'hôtel [mehtr doh-tel]
Buttery white sauce with chopped parsley and lemon juice.

Marchand de vin
Demi-glace reduced with sautéed shallots and red wine.

Maltaise [mal-tehz]
Hollandaise with rind and juice of blood oranges.

Mandelkren [*mahn*-del-krehn]
Horseradish sauce with almonds.

Maréchale [ma-reh-shal]
A *velouté* with mushroom purée.

Marengo
Tomatoes sautéed in oil, or *sauce chausseur*, with mushrooms and truffles, onions and garlic.

Marigny [ma-ree-nyee]
Demi-glace boiled with white wine, mushroom stock, and tomato purée.

Marinière [ma-ree-nyair]

List of sauces (continued)

Sauce Bercy with mussel stock and egg yolk.

Mayonnaise
Olive oil and egg yolk whipped together, with vinegar, mustard, salt, and pepper.

Medici [*meh*-dee-chee]
Sauce béarnaise with red wine and tomato purée.

Meunière [meu-nyair]
Browned butter with lemon juice and parsley.

Mirabeau [meer-a-boh]
Sauce allemande with garlic and herb butter.

Mornay [mor-neh]
Cheese sauce, usually *béchamel* enriched with butter, yolks, and cheese.

Mousseline [moos-leen]
Hollandaise lightened with whipped cream or egg white.

Nantua
Cream sauce with crayfish butter, basically, but also a *mirepoix* browned in better with crayfish, then flamed in Cognac, moistened with white wine and fish essence, then cooked with tomatoes, fish *velouté*, salt and cayenne.

Napoletana [nah-po-leh-*tah*-nah]
A classic Italian sauce made by reducing chopped onion and ham sautéed in butter, to which has been added veal stock, Marsala, bay, thyme, cloves, pepper, and mushroom, then combining this with meat sauce, tomato sauce, and more rich stock, these three having been reduced together. Serve with *pasta*, and red wines like Gragnano or Vulture.

Napolitaine [na-pol-ee-tehn]
Reduction of *mirepoix*, Marsala, and tomatoes, with *demiglace*; or oil and lemon juice with garlic and parsley.

Newburgh
Sliced lobster warmed in butter with salt and cayenne, moistened with Sherry or Madeira, reduced, and bound with yolks and cream.

Normande [nor-mahnd]
Fish *velouté* boiled with fish essence, mushroom essence and

oyster liquid, bound with yolks and cream, reduced, then finished with butter and cream.

Norvégienne [nor-veh-zhen]
Hard-boiled yolks, beaten with mustard, oil, and vinegar.

Oberskren [*oh*-bers-krehn]
Cream sauce with horseradish and paprika.

Orientale [oh-ree-on-tal]
Sauce américaine with curry.

Paloise [pal-wahz]
Sauce béarnaise with mint instead of tarragon.

Paprika
Sauté of onions with paprika, veal glaze, cream or sour cream.

Parisienne [pa-ree-zyen]
Brown sauce with a reduction of shallots.

Périgueux [peh-ree-guh]
Demi-glace with truffle essence and diced truffle.

Périgourdine [peh-ree-goor-deen]
Demi-glace with puréed foie gras, diced truffle.

Persil [per-seel]
Parsley in a *velouté* or butter sauce.

Piquante
Chopped shallots reduced in wine and vinegar, with *demi-glace*, chopped gherkins, parsley, chervil, tarragon.

Poivrade
Mirepoix sauté, with crushed peppercorns and *bouquet garni*, reduced in vinegar and white wine, then with *demi-glace*, strained and finished with butter. English version adds currant jelly.

Polignac [poh-lee-nyak]
White wine sauce with mushroom julienne.

Polonaise [po-lo-nehz]
A *velouté* with horseradish and lemon juice, and with sour cream or *demi-glace*.

Pondicherry
Thickened veal stock with tomato purée, and curry or green peppers.

List of sauces (continued)

Portugaise [por-tü-ghehz]
Tomato sauce reduced with veal glaze, onions, garlic and chopped parsley.

Poulette [poo-let]
Sauce allemande with mushroom essence, then lemon juice and chopped parsley.

Princesse [pran-ses]
A white sauce, often with crayfish, or parsley.

Printanière [pran-tan-yair]
Sauce allemande with green vegetable purée.

Provençale [pro-vahn-sal]
Diced tomatoes sautéed in olive oil, with garlic and chopped parsley. Browned mushrooms often added.

Ravigote [ra-vee-goht]
Oil and vinegar with *fines herbes*, onions, and capers or reduction of wine and vinegar with *velouté* and shallot butter, with chopped chervil, chives, tarragon.

Régence [reh-zhahns]
Various basic sauces reduced with Rhine wine and truffle and mushroom peel, strained, then finished with truffle essence.

Reine, à la [ren]
Sauce suprême with almond butter or whipped cream.

Rémoulade [reh-moo-lod]
Mayonnaise with mustard, chopped herbs, capers, anchovy essence.

Riche [reesh]
Sauce diplomate, lobster cream sauce.

Richelieu [reesh-lyeu]
Enriched *sauce allemande* with a sauté of onion, or *demi-glace* with Madeira or tomato sauce.

Robert [roh-bair] or **Rowboat**
Brown onion sauce. Sauté of onions reduced with wine and vinegar, *demi-glace* and mustard being added.

Romaine
Sauce espagnole with pine nuts, currants, and sultanas.

List of sauces (continued)

Rouennaise [roo-on-nehz]
Sauce madère or *bordelaise* with raw duck liver purée.

Royale [rwah-yal]
Sauce suprême with Sherry and butter.

Russe [rüs]
Sauce allemande with sour cream, horseradish and vinegar, or mayonnaise with purée of lobster and caviar spiced with mustard and Escoffier sauce.

St. Malo [san ma-loh]
White wine sauce with mustard, a reduction of shallots, and anchovy butter.

St. Menehould [muh-nuh-oo]
Cream sauce enriched with veal glaze, chopped mushrooms, and parsley.

Saxonne [sa-son]
Butter sauce with a reduction of shallots and fish stock, with mustard and lemon juice or rind.

Sévillane [seh-veel-lan]
Demi-glace with purée of tomato and pimiento.

Soffritto [sof-*freet*-toh]
A sauce of diced pork and chicken livers, tomatoes and green peppers, for *pasta*. Serve with local reds or whites.

Soubise [soo-beez]
Cream sauce with onion purée.

Suédoise [sweh-dwahz]
Mayonnaise with horseradish and applesauce.

Suprême [sü-prem]
A basic sauce, thickened chicken stock enriched with fresh cream.

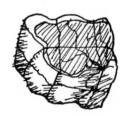

Tartare
Mayonnaise with hard-boiled yolks, chopped onions, and chives, often capers and gherkins.

Talleyrand [tal-leh-rahn]
Enriched chicken stock with cream and Madeira.

Tomate [toh-mat]
Tomato paste to which is added *mirepoix* and bacon browned in butter; this is reduced in the oven, where it is sprinkled with flour, then are added stock, garlic, a *bouquet garni*, salt, sugar, and peppercorns, with some butter at the end.

Toulouse [too-looz]
Sauce allemande reduced with mushroom and truffle essence.

Trianon [tree-a-nawn]
Mayonnaise with purées of onion and tomato, chopped gherkin and pimiento.

Tyrolienne [tih-rohl-yen]
Hollandaise or mayonnaise with tomato purée, or tomatoed *sauce béarnaise* with olive oil added.

Valéria [va-lehr-ya]
Sauce bordelaise with mustard, horseradish and chervil.

Valois [val-wah]
Béarnaise with meat glaze.

Velouté [vuh-loo-tay]
Velvet sauce is made by adding *roux* to various stocks simply to thicken them: *velouté de veau* is based on white stock; *velouté de volaille* (voh-ly-uh) is based on chicken stock; *velouté de poisson* (pwah-sohn) is based on fish stock; *velouté de légumes* (leh-güm) is based on vegetable stock.

Vénétienne [veh-neh-syen]
White wine sauce thickened with cream and yolks mixed with parsley, or reduced herb vinegar, strained, then finished with green herb butter, chopped tarragon and chervil.

Verte [vairt]
Mayonnaise with blanched green herbs.

Victoria
Sauce suprême with lobster butter and truffles.

List of sauces (continued)

Villageoise [veel-azh-wahz]
Sauce velouté enriched with onion, and veal and mushroom stocks, bound with yolks, cream, and butter.

Villeroi [veel-rwah]
A coating sauce from *sauce allemande* that is reduced with ham or truffle essence, to which onion or tomato purée can be added.

Vincent [van-sahn]
Mayonnaise or tartar sauce, with green herb purée and mashed hard-boiled eggs.

Vinaigrette [vee-neh-gret]
Oil and vinegar mixture seasoned with salt and pepper, chopped parsley and tarragon, chervil and chives, often onions and capers.

White sauce
A milk sauce thickened with *roux.*

White wine sauce
A fish *velouté* or stock with white wine.

Yorkshire
Brown sauce with Port and orange peel or juice.

Zingara
Demi-glace or *espagnole* with tomato purée and julienne of ham, tongue, and truffles.

Zouave [zwahv]
Demi-glace with tomato purée, mustard, garlic, and tarragon.

Sauerbraten [*zow*-er-brah-tn]
Beef pot roast first pickled for at least two days in a boiled vinegar marinade seasoned with pepper, bay, cloves, onions, carrots, and celery, then braised. Traditionally served with potato pancakes or dumplings, red cabbage, stewed prunes, beer.

Saumon du chapeau rouge [so-mawn dü shah-po roozh]
Salmon, like trout, seems to taste best when simply broiled or poached, as is usual on the Loire; but around Bordeaux slices are browned with onions, carrots, and herbs, then moistened with red wine, baked, and served with sautéed mushrooms and

leeks; in Gascony, salmon is browned in olive oil then braised in white wine, with leeks. Serve with dry or flowery white wines like Graves, Chablis, or Rhine wines.

Saure Hachsen [*zow*-ruh *hok*-sen]
Veal knuckle parboiled in a vinegar stock, then drained and simmered in stock with sliced root vegetables, sprinkled with parsley, and served with beer.

Scaloppine alla Marsala [skah-lop-*pee*-neh *ah*-lah mar-*sah*-lah]
Thin slices of veal, used in various ways like chops, usually pounded, then floured and cooked quickly in butter, Marsala being added to the pan juice at the last minute, this being poured over the veal, along with a squirt of lemon juice; *alla bolognese* (boh-lo-*nyeh*-zeh) is with ham and potato slices, baked in the oven with a meat sauce and Parmesan cheese; *alla fiorentina* (fyor-en-*tee*-nah) is with spinach and cream sauce. Serve with dry white wines like Soave or Orvieto, or even Vernaccia.

Scampi alla cardinale [*skahm*-pee *ahl*-lah car-dee-*nah*-leh]
Scampi are salt-water crayfish, the French *langoustine*, like our giant shrimp, wrapped in ham and browned in oil, then served with a spicy cream sauce. They are served with a variety of sauces, and are often grilled. Serve with dry white Soave or Orvieto.

Schwäbische Kalbsvögel [*shvay*-bih-shuh kahlps-*feu*-ghel]
"Swabian veal birds" are pounded veal slices spread with forcemeat and bacon, then rolled and braised on sautéed root vegetables, onions, and herbs in brown stock and white wine. Served with the reduced stock to which anchovies and capers are added, with beer.

Selle d'agneau basquaise [sell dan-yo bas-kehz]
Buttered saddle of lamb roasted over a wood fire and served with *sauce béarnaise*, to which peppermint has been added, served with potatoes sautéed with almonds. Accompany with a fine red Bordeaux.

Serbisches Reisfleisch   [*zehr*-bish-es *rys*-flysh]
An Austrian rice mold, made by browning cubes of veal,
chopped onions, and bacon in butter, then adding rice, paprika,
and stock. Serve with Austrian whites, light reds.

Sesos españolas   [*say*-sohs es-pan-*yo*-lahs]
Brains, diced and sautéed with chopped parsley in butter laced
with lemon, then put into pastry shells and masked with cream
sauce and grated cheese. Serve with a dry or flowery Rioja, or
Alella.

Sfoglie in saor   [*sfohl*-yeh een sah-*or*]
A Venetian specialty, sole marinated in vinegar and onions,
raisins and pine nuts, then dredged and sautéed. Serve with dry
white Prosecco or Termeno.

Sogliola al piatto   [*sohl*-yo-lah ahl *pyaht*-to]
Sole filets are prepared in Puglia in this simple way to bring
out the delicacy of the fish—the filets are sprinkled with
minced garlic, parsley, salt, and olive oil, then covered and
placed over boiling water so that they steam, and are served
with slices of lemon; *alla veneziana* (veh-*neh*-tsee-ah-nah) is
sole rubbed with a mixture of butter, chopped mint, parsley
and garlic, then served with a white wine and onion sauce.
Serve with dry white wines like Soave or Prosecco.

Sole Normande   [sohl nor-mahnd]
The most popular fish of France, served with hundreds of
sauces and garnishes, and usually poached because of its deli-

cacy, generally tastes best when served in the fashion of the Atlantic coast. The dish is cooked in cream in a closed dish—although certain versions call for poaching the sole in butter and cider—with mussels, shrimp, mushrooms and oysters; *dieppoise* (dyep-pwahz) is served with mussels and shrimp in a white wine sauce. Sole calls for light wines like Muscadet or Graves, but any good white wine accents the dish.

Soufflés [soo-flay]
Soufflés of mashed fish or fowl, or melted cheese—blended with separately beaten yolks and whites and combined with a white sauce, then baked in the oven—are among the most delicate and delightful of dishes. They are generally accompanied with Champagne or full white wines, dry or flowery, particularly Burgundies and Rhine wines from the Rheingau or Rheinpfalz.

Spaghetti alla carbonara [spah-*ghet*-tee *ahl*-lah car-bo-*nah*-rah]
Spaghetti served with a sauce made by lightly sautéing juliennes of ham, bacon, and mushroom in oil and butter, then taking this off the fire and adding Pecorino cheese and two beaten eggs; *alla bolognese* (bo-lo-*nyeh*-zeh) is with the famous meat and tomato sauce; *alla carrettiera* (kah-ret-*tyehr*-ah) is tuna fish, fried mushroom and tomato sauce; *alla matriciana* (mah-tree-*chah*-nah) is salt pork, onion, green pepper, and tomato sauce; *alla siciliana* (see-chee-*lyah*-nah) is with eggplant and tomatoes, green peppers and capers, olives and anchovies; *alla spoletina* (spoh-leh-*tee*-nah) is truffles pounded with anchovies, garlic, and parsley thinned with oil, water and tomato paste. Serve with dry whites like Capri, or reds like Grignolino.

Spiedini [spyeh-*dee*-nee]
Broiled or braised skewered chunks of veal, sausage, and bacon, liberally sprinkled with sage. Serve with any light red or white wine, like Valtellina or Verdicchio.

Spiessbraten [*shpees*-brah-tn]
Rolled ribs of beef rubbed with salt, pepper, and dry mustard, then roasted on a spit over an oak fire. In Frankfurt, this

specialty is also rubbed with onion, sometimes sprinkled with clove, and served with a sauce based on sour cream and the drippings. Serve with beer.

Stoccafisso [stok-kah-*fees*-so]
A hearty Genoese specialty, dried cod is soaked in milk and oil with anchovies and walnuts, then served with black olives; *alla livornese* (lee-vor-*neh*-zeh), with tripe and tomatoes, onions, celery, and carrots in oil and white wine; *alla marchignana* (mar-kee-*nyah*-nah) is with oil and tomato sauce, seasoned with anchovies and garlic, parsley and rosemary. Serve with beer or local dry white wines.

Stock
Stock is the boiled-down cooking water from beef or veal, fowl or fish, which is the basis for many sauces, or which is used as a fortified liquid in which many preparations, such as eggs, *pasta*, and vegetables, are cooked.

Stockfish
Boned cod dried in the air, which is soaked in water before being boiled or poached, after which it is used with a variety of sauces and casserole dishes. Serve with white wines like Puilly-Fuissé.

Stufatino [stoo-fah-*tee*-no]
Braised veal, with white wine, rosemary, and Italian tomatoes; *alla romana* is a stew of beef and red wine with browned onions and garlic, oregano or marjoram, diced bacon and tomato paste, with enough water to cover. Serve with Chianti or Sangiovese.

Stufato di manzo genovese [stoo-*fah*-to dee *mahn*-zo jen-oh-*veh*-zeh]
This Genoan pot roast is beef braised in dry white wine with fresh basil and sliced onion, tomato, carrot, and celery. Serve with red Lambrusco or Barbaresco.

Supplì di riso al telefono [soop-*plee* dee *ree*-zo ahl teh-*leh*-fo-no]
Rice croquettes filled with mozzarella or provatura cheese, fried in oil, so-called because the cheese strings when the croquette is

bitten into. In Rome, a chicken-and-tomato ragout is used for filling, elsewhere chopped meat and cheese. Serve with beer or local dry red or white wines.

Suprême de volaille   [soo-prem duh vo-ly]
Chicken breasts served with a variety of sauces and garnishes. Accompany with light reds of Bordeaux or Burgundy.

Tacchino ripieno   [tahk-*kee*-no ree-*pyeh*-no]
Stuffed roasted turkey is a great specialty of northern Italy, particularly in Milan, where the redolent stuffing is made not only of giblets, ham, and sausage, but also includes chestnuts, prunes, and apples, along with truffles, onions, Parmesan cheese, nutmeg, and pepper, all bound with eggs and white wine. There are other versions of turkey, which is used in dishes that were originally made from chicken, but none approaches this one. Serve with a noble red Barolo or Gattinara, or a white Soave.

Tagliatelle verdi   [tahl-yah-*tehl*-leh *vehr*-dee]
Thin egg noodles colored green by adding spinach purée during the making, served with a variety of sauces. Serve with white wines like Soave.

Tartufi alla piemontese   [tar-*too*-fee *ahl*-la pyeh-mohn-*teh*-zeh]
One of the great specialties of the Piedmont, white truffles cooked in the classic Piedmont sauce, *bagna cauda*, then served with croutons. Serve with Cortese, white and dry, or any dry red, like Barolo or Gattinara.

Terrine de Nérac   [tair-reen duh nay-rack]
This town near Bordeaux is famous for its loaves of meat and fowl, made by lining a pan with fat bacon and filling it with layers of spicy meats and forcemeats, topping it with more fat bacon, poaching it in the oven in a water bath, and serving it cold, to be sliced. Accompany with red Bordeaux or white Graves.

Torta pasqualina   [*tor*-tah pahs-kwah-*lee*-nah]
A sort of pie that is an Easter specialty in Genoa, layers of pastry stuffed with artichoke, spinach, and other greens, often

peas and beets, bound with egg and milk and cheese. Serve
with a dry white like Vermentino or dry Cinque Terre.

Tortellini alla bolognese [tor-teh-*lee*-nee *ahl*-lah bo-lo-*nyeh*-zeh]
Small *pasta* tubes stuffed with ground pork, chicken, and ham
or sausage, and Parmesan cheese, bound with egg and seasoned
with salt and nutmeg, boiled in broth, in which they are often
served. Serve with white wines like Soave or Albana.

Tortilla española [tor-*teel*-yah]
Spanish omelet is one with tomatoes, cooked by turning over,
rather than rolling. A version, *la frita* (*free*-tah), includes
cooked onions and grated cheese. The traditional Spanish tortilla is invariably served flat, browned on both sides. Serve with
white Rioja, dry or flowery.

Tortino di carciofi [tor-*tee*-no dee kar-*cho*-fee]
This baked omelet with baby artichokes is a Florentine classic,
made by browning thin slices of artichoke in oil and butter,
then pouring over them eggs beaten with a fork and baking
this for ten minutes in a moderate oven: *tortino d'uova nella
neve* (*dwoh*-vah *nel*-lah *neh*-veh), baked "eggs in snow," is
made by spreading a layer of mashed potato in a dish, covering
this with thin slices of mozzarella, making indentations with a
spoon in the base and breaking eggs in these, then sprinkling
with grated Parmesan, dotting with butter, and baking in a
hot oven. Serve with a dry white wine like Orvieto or Verdicchio.

Tournedos [toor-nuh-doh]
A thick slice of the tenderloin, one of the tenderest steak cuts,

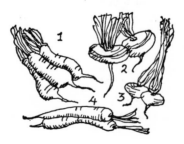

generally grilled and served on fried toast, with a sauce and a variety of garnishes. Serve with red wines like Nuits-St.-Georges or St. Émilion.

Tourte à la viande   [toort ah lah vee-ahnd]
Meat pies, eaten hot or cold, are excellent with all red wines and dry whites, particularly this mixture of chopped veal and pork that is marinated in white wine and Cognac before baking; this one is usually served hot.

Tranche de tête d'aloyau   [trahnsh duh tet dah-loy-oh]
The rump steak, cut thick and prepared like a sirloin, accompanied with full red wines like Burgundy.

Trenette al pesto   [treh-*net*-teh ahl *pehs*-to]
These shoelacelike noodles are a Genoese specialty when served with *il pesto*, the famous basil sauce. Serve with white Cinque Terre or Soave.

Triglia alla livornese   [*treel*-yah *ahl*-lah lee-vor-*neh*-zeh]
Red mullet is dredged in flour, then browned in oil. A seasoned white wine and tomato sauce is poured over, with chopped basil and parsley sprinkled on top. Serve with a dry white like Soave or Cinque Terre.

Tripe à la mode de Caen   [treep ah lah maud duh kan]
This way of preparing tripe has gone a long way from the Norman town where it began, and the classic method is often varied. The tripe is simply braised for half-a-dozen hours or so in cider laced with Calvados, the separated meat and bones from a calf's foot and a steer's foot being laid on a bed of chopped onions and carrots in a casserole, the tripe slices being laid on these, with garlic, leeks and a *bouquet garni* that accents thyme and laurel, the dish being sealed with a flour paste cover so the tripe will stay white. The nearby town of *Ferté-Macé* prepares tripe by omitting the cider and braising the tripe all night in butter and Calvados. South of Brittany, around Angoulême, white wine and bouillon, with plenty of spices, are used. White wines like Graves or Muscadet are often served.

Trippa alla fiorentina [*treep*-pah *ahl*-lah fyor-ehn-*tee*-nah]
Tripe is a favorite Italian dish, cooked in Florence with a meat
sauce, marjoram, and Parmesan cheese; *alla romana* is with a
meat and tomato sauce flavored with mint and grated cheese;
alla siennese (syen-*eh*-zeh) with sausages and saffron. Serve
with red wines like Chianti or Sangiovese.

Trote in salsa d'acciughe [*troh*-teh een *sahl*-sah dahch-*choo*-
gheh]
Trout browned in olive oil, served with a sauce made of anchovy butter, Marsala, and white wine, to which chopped mint,
parsley, and lemon juice are added. Serve with a white wine
like Capri or Soave.

Truffes sous la cendre [trüf soo lah sahn-druh]
"Truffles under the ashes" are an unmatched delicacy. They
are seasoned, dribbled with Cognac, wrapped in salt pork and
then wet paper, and thrust into the ashes to bake. A more
elaborate, but less elemental, way is to add a slice of *foie gras*,
then wrap the whole in dough. Truffles seem to have little
taste by themselves, but their essence can be divined when
served this way, with a glass of fine red Burgundy or Bordeaux.

Truite au bleu [trweet oh bleu]
The firm-fleshed and delicate trout calls for the simplest of
cooking—quick broiling or pan-frying—and the flavor is often
lost when it is masked with sauces. For blue trout, the cleaned
fish is quickly poached in water, bouillon, or white wine, with
vinegar, and served with melted butter; in Burgundy, and elsewhere, red wine is sometimes used: *meunière* calls for dredging
the trout with flour and sautéing it quickly in butter, with
lemon juice and parsley, often with almonds; *en papillote* (on
pah-pee-yot) calls for wrapping it in buttered paper, with
chopped shallots, then baking. Serve with dry or flowery wines
like Chablis, Traminer, or Rhine wines.

Turbot à la Saint Malo [tur-bo ah lah san mah-lo]
Turbot is a flat, halibutlike fish that is prepared like sole, and
often poached in white wine or bouillon, but in Brittany it is

generally simply grilled and served with a white wine sauce, and served with Muscadet or other dry or flowery white wines.

Uccelletti [oo-chel-*let*-tee]
This Florentine favorite is larks or other small birds roasted on a spit and flavored with laurel; they are so popular that *uccelletti scappati* (skahp-*pah*-tee), rolled veal birds, and sausages, bits of pork and liver, are similarly grilled and served with bits of toast; *alla Maremma* (mah-*rem*-mah) is made by browning these birds in a sauce of garlic and anchovies, with tomatoes, peppers, and olives. Serve with red wine like Chianti.

Veau farci [vo far-see]
A filet, breast, or shoulder of veal stuffed with chopped herbs and mushrooms, pork, bacon, and chicken livers, browned, then braised in white wine and bouillon with celery and onions stuck with cloves. Generally served with sautéed mushrooms and light red wines like Médoc or Beaune.

Vermicelli alla bolognese [vehr-mee-*chehl*-lee *ahl*-lah bo-lo-*nyeh*-zeh]
Very fine spaghettilike *pasta*, particularly notable when served with the celebrated meat and tomato sauce of Bologna, or a clam sauce. Serve with reds like Sangiovese or Lambrusco, or whites like Soave.

Vincisgrassi [veen-chees-*grahs*-see]
A stout and famous dish of the Marches, layers of *lasagne*, between which is a sauce of veal and ham, giblets, and chicken breast, mushrooms and truffles, giblets and tomato paste, all bound with creamed chicken broth, the casserole being baked in the oven. Serve with white Verdicchio or red Sangiovese.

Vitello all'uccelletto [vee-*tehl*-lo ahl-looch-chehl-*let*-to]
Thin veal scallops, dredged in flour and browned quickly in oil and butter, with crumbled bay leaves and garlic or sage added, along with white wine and a little stock or tomato paste, which is reduced, and finished quickly with butter and chopped

parsley, the entire operation taking less than five minutes. Serve with a light red Bardolino or Sangiovese, or a white Soave.

Vitello tonnato [vee-*tehl*-lo tohn-*nah*-to]
One of the greatest of cold dishes, and a Milanese specialty, thin slices of braised or roasted cold veal, served with a cold oil and lemon sauce containing pounded tuna and anchovies, plus capers. Serve with a full dry white wine like Orvieto or Soave.

Vol-au-vent [vohl-oh-vahn]
"Flight-in-the-wind" is the name for light pastry shells filled with bits of fowl, fish, sea food, or tasty bits of meat, in a cream sauce, the kind of dish from which came chicken à la king. Serve with light wines, like Graves reds or whites.

Vongole alla siciliana [*vohn*-go-leh *ahl*-lah see-cheel-*yah*-nah]
Mussels steamed with olive oil, garlic, and parsley. Serve with dry white Capri or Vernaccia.

Waterzooi [vah-ter-zooy]
A Flemish specialty, fresh-water fish stewed in water or stock to which a *bouquet garni*, butter, and chopped celery have been added, the sauce finally thickened with bread crumbs. There is also a chicken *waterzooi*, leeks and onions stuck with cloves being added to the stock. Serve with white wines like Meursault or Rhines.

Zucchini ripieni [tsook-*kee*-nee ree-*pyeh*-nee]
Boiled zucchini, stuffed with their own pulp mixed with ham and bacon, mushrooms and oregano, Parmesan and bread crumbs, bound with a cream sauce, then baked in the oven. Serve with white wines like Soave.

Zuppa alla pavese [*tsoop*-pah *ahl*-lah pah-*veh*-zeh]
This luncheon soup is meat broth poured boiling over two yolks set on a slice of toast in the bottom of a bowl; *alla marinara* or *di pesci* (*pesh*-ee) is almost a fish stew that varies with the local varieties; *rustica* (*roos*-tee-kah) contains beans,

potatoes, sausages, and so forth. Serve with white wines like Frascati or Sansevero.

Zwiebelfleisch [*tzvee*-bel-flysh]
Sliced beef and onions, browned then stewed in beef stock, usually served with dumplings, and Austrian whites or light reds.

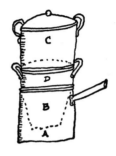